The Story of Mexico

Cortés and the Spanish Conquest

The Story of Mexico

Cortés and the Spanish Conquest

R. Conrad Stein

MORGAN REYNOLDS
PUBLISHING

Greensboro, North Carolina

The Story of Mexico

THE STORY OF MEXICO
CORTÉS AND THE SPANISH CONQUEST
Copyright © 2008 by R. Conrad Stein

Library of Congress Cataloging-in-Publication Data

Stein, R. Conrad.
    The story of Mexico. The Spanish conquest / by R. Conrad Stein.
      p. cm.
    Includes bibliographical references and index.
    ISBN-13: 978-1-59935-053-0
    ISBN-10: 1-59935-053-X
    1. Mexico--History--Conquest, 1519-1540--Juvenile literature. I. Title. II.
Title: Spanish conquest.
    F1230.S85 2007
    972'.02--dc22
                                        2007016004

Printed in the United States of America
First Edition

For my wife Deborah and daughter, Janna

Contents

Cortés and his men entering Mexico *(Courtesy of British Library)*

ONE

City of Dreams

November 8, 1519. For almost three months the Spanish army marched relentlessly toward the capital of the Aztec nation (today's Mexico City). The soldiers trekked over dizzying mountains whose peaks pierced the clouds. They passed through muddy villages as well as through large towns with pyramids and temples rising in their centers. The men from Europe fought bloody battles with the people of America as they pushed toward their goal—a fabulous city called Tenochtitlán.

The Spaniards were adventurers who came to the Americas seeking riches. By 1519 Spanish soldiers of fortune had lived in the New World for about fifteen years. So far their quest for treasure had been a bitter disappointment. They crossed the ocean lured by tales of fantastic societies that existed on the other side. The societies were said to be so rich that even their lowliest peasants ate from solid gold plates. Then, after braving an Atlantic crossing, the foreigners settled on islands

A conquistador with horses

in the Caribbean Sea where they encountered primitive peoples whose only gold consisted of a few pieces of jewelry.

The men marching through central Mexico hoped this city of the Aztecs would contain the treasure trove of their dreams. Even the land changed as they traveled. The mountain peaks they crossed were barren and windswept. Then the path dropped into a broad green valley of tall pine forests, shining lakes, and lush cornfields. Villages in the valley were made up of stone houses whose white plastered walls gleamed like silver when seen from a distance.

Despite their high expectations, every Spaniard was painfully aware of the grave dangers he faced. Their force numbered about four hundred foot soldiers and fifteen horsemen. Many thousands of native warriors, who hated the Aztecs, marched with the Spaniards and served as their allies. This

The Spanish hoped to reach the city of Tenochtitlan, which they believed held unparalleled riches.

Spanish-led army was puny compared to the Aztecs, who could put more than 100,000 men in the field at a moment's notice. Aztecs were famed in Mexico as tough, disciplined fighters who were fearless in battle.

The trail bent at a hill, and suddenly the soldiers saw the outskirts of the capital. A wave of excitement rippled through the ranks as they marched closer. Rising before them was a gleaming island city perched in the middle of a great lake. The Spaniards looked in wonder at the arrow-straight streets, the broad canals, and the mighty pyramids and castles. It appeared to be a fantasy land, a place created not by men but by angels. Said one Spaniard, "we were amazed and said that it was like the enchantments they tell of in the legend[s] . . . And some of our soldiers even asked whether the things that we saw were not a dream."

The meeting which loomed between the Aztecs and the Spaniards would be unique in history. Here, facing each other, stood two advanced civilizations which rose on opposite sides of an ocean 4,000 miles wide. Both developed their own religious beliefs, their own art and architecture, their

An Aztec jaguar warrior, one of the elite soldiers of the Aztec army

own literature, and their own codes of conduct. Each society knew almost nothing of the other. Now the two peoples had a chance either to wage war or to exchange ideas peacefully. Their encounter would put the human character itself on trial.

TWO

The Aztec World

A legend believed by all Aztecs claimed the people once lived in a marvelous land called Aztlán which was far to the north. Atzlán was a Garden of Eden where fruit trees grew and birds and fish splashed in sparkling lakes. An ancient text said, "There [in Aztlán] they feasted on great numbers of ducks of all kinds . . . They enjoyed the melodic songs of red-and-yellow-headed birds. They gorged themselves on a variety of great and beautiful fish."

Somehow the Aztec people angered a powerful god. The legend does not give details as to exactly how they displeased the deity. As in the Biblical story of Adam and Eve, the god expelled the Aztecs from their paradise of Aztlán. For generations the Aztecs wandered the deserts of northern Mexico. Water was scarce. For food they ate snakes, lizards, and even spiders. Still, these desert nomads had hope. During their journeys they adopted a god called Huitzilopochtli (pronounced heet-zee-loh-POHS-tlee). In the Aztec language

The Aztecs depart from Aztlán.

the name meant Hummingbird of the Left. Huitzilopochtli promised the Aztecs that one day they would find a home and become a mighty nation. The Hummingbird gave them one specific instruction: as they wandered they should always keep the Gulf of Mexico (the Atlantic Ocean) toward their left hand. For that reason the god was called Hummingbird of the Left.

Following the god's instructions the Aztec people moved out of northern Mexico, pushing steadily south. In the 1200s, the tribe drifted into the fertile Valley of Mexico. That valley, which is about sixty miles long and forty miles wide, contains the richest soil in central Mexico. Present-day Mexico City lies on the valley's southern tip. The Aztecs were impressed

The Aztecs worshipped the god Huitzilopochtli, whose name translates to "Hummingbird of the Left."

by the rich valley, filled with tall forests and sparkling lakes. The wanderers also admired the towns they saw, built of stone houses and boasting great temples.

At one time a people called the Toltecs rose to prominence in the Valley of Mexico. They were a nation of poets, artists, and warriors. For four hundred years the Toltecs ruled the valley and most of central Mexico. Toltec farmers raised bountiful crops of corn, beans, and chili peppers. Their workers built a string of impressive cities.

Teotihuacán

Also in the Valley of Mexico were the ruins of a fabulous city with two tall pyramids. The Aztecs entered this city when it was already one thousand years old and was long abandoned. They could not believe the place was built by human beings. It was simply too grandiose to be created by the hands of mortals. The Aztecs named the city Teotihuacán (The Place Where Men Become Gods). In about 400 AD Teotihuacán held 200,000 people, making it one of the world's largest cities at the time. By 700 AD the city was devoid of people and its impressive buildings stood like forlorn ghosts. No one knows why the original inhabitants left the city.

Teotihuacán lays only a forty-five-minute bus ride from modern Mexico City. It is Mexico's most visited archaeological site. Tourists today climb the steps of the pyramids and ponder the mysteries of their surroundings: Why did ancient people gather here? Why did they suddenly leave their marvelous city?

As newcomers, the Aztecs were not liked by the established nations in the valley. Civilized people regarded the Aztecs as barbarians who lacked manners and were thought to be cruel and treacherous. One ancient scribe wrote, "And when the [Aztecs] arrived here . . . they were the very last to come into the Valley, and nobody knew of them or welcomed them . . . and they were turned away from every village."

The Aztecs camped in places where no one else wanted to live. Their first settlement was on dusty Chapultepec Hill (Grasshopper Hill). A prince then allowed the Aztecs to live in a region infested with rattlesnakes. The prince hoped that starvation and the snakes would finish off this pesky tribe. To the prince's astonishment the Aztecs thrived by eating the snakes. In an even more shocking development, the Aztecs killed the prince's only daughter as part of their religious ceremonies.

By the time the Aztecs came, the Toltecs had lost their dominance in the Valley of Mexico. Politically the Valley was made up of six major city-states which were almost constantly at war with each other. This situation played into Aztec fortunes and gave them employment.

Centuries of wandering in the deserts made the people accustomed to hardships. Also their status as outcasts gave the Aztecs greater unity than neighboring tribes. Since they were hated by all others, the Aztecs were forced to band together as a strong family. Toughness and fierce loyalties to each other molded the Aztec army into a force that was almost unbeatable. The Aztecs became mercenaries, soldiers who fought for pay. No one liked or trusted the Aztecs, but the various city-states were willing to pay them to fight their battles.

While they fought as mercenaries, the Aztecs continued to search for a permanent home. In their quest they remained guided by their chief god Huitzilopochtli, the Hummingbird. Priests carried a wooden statue of the hummingbird deity in

Painting of Aztec warriors

a cagelike device as the tribe roamed the Valley of Mexico. By observing special rituals, the priests claimed they could speak with the Hummingbird. The god instructed the priests to look for a place where they would see a magical sign: an eagle sitting on a cactus while eating a snake. On that spot they should build a city. That city would serve as the capital of a new Aztec nation, and that nation would become the most powerful on earth.

According to Aztec records the promise of the god was delivered in the year 1325. On an island in the middle of Lake Texcoco the people saw the eagle, the cactus, and the snake. Immediately they began constructing a city which they called Tenochtitlán (Place of the Cactus).

An Aztec depiction of the founding of Tenochtitlan

Now that they were settled, the genius of the Aztec people burst forth. They were not innovators. They freely borrowed ideas from others. However the Aztecs refined the techniques of others to create marvels in engineering and art that became unique to Aztec society.

Their promised city began as a muddy little island in the middle of the broad but shallow Lake Texcoco. Aztec workers expanded this island base by pounding timbers into the lake bottom and then dumping soil between the timbers and the island shore. Thus the island grew in rings, like the trunk of a tree. As the island expanded Aztec engineers created canals which allowed boats to carry goods. Using canals was not a new concept in the Americas. But Aztec canals were ruler-straight. Streets paved with mud-dried brick were built paralleling each canal. The canal-street system created a sense of beauty and order unknown in other ancient American cities.

> ## Legendary Foundations
>
> The miracle of the cactus is still important in Mexican culture. The year 1325, when the Aztecs claimed they first saw their vision, is recognized as the founding date of Mexico City, the nation's capital. Also, a picture of an eagle sitting on a cactus while eating a snake is the center symbol on every Mexican flag.
>
>
>
> Mexican flag

The Aztecs took great pains to prevent pollution of the Lake Texcoco's waters. Human wastes were collected and shipped to farms on the mainland to be used as fertilizer. Still the waters of the lake were never clean enough to drink,

A map of the Lake Texcoco area from 1847

and they had a salt content. To accommodate their need for water, the Aztecs built one of the finest aqueducts ever seen in the Americas. The aqueduct consisted of two parallel pipes made from stone and wood which took water from springs on Chapultepec Hill and ran it three miles to the island city. The pipes stood on beams perched high over the lake. The beams allowed fishing boats and freight-hauling boats to easily pass underneath the aqueduct.

To feed the ever-expanding population the Aztecs grew crops on chinampas, or floating gardens. Lake Texcoco sits in the lowest spot of the Valley of Mexico. Its waters cannot be channeled and gravity-fed to farms to provide irrigation. So, rather than bringing water to land, the chinampa system

Aztec farmers work on their chinampas.

allowed farmers to bring land to water. Chinampas were constructed by sinking retaining walls into the lake and filling
the walls with soil taken from the lake's bottom. Farmers
planted their crops on the surface of these artificial islands.
For irrigation, lake waters were allowed to seep through the
retaining walls and onto the surface of the fields. To provide
strength, trees were planted along the edges of the chinampas.
Trees and growing crops made the chinampas look like floating gardens. In sunny central Mexico chinampas regularly
produced two and sometimes three harvests a year.

Xochimilco

A floating island at a spot called Xochimilco serves as a tourist
attraction and provides flowers for modern Mexico City. Xochimilco
is the only remaining chinampa in the Valley of Mexico.

The Aztecs remained a military society. Work on their many projects proceeded in a disciplined manner. Armies of laborers toiled endlessly without complaint. Because of Aztec discipline and the skill of their engineers and artists, a monumental city grew in Lake Texcoco.

Great pyramids with flat tops rose in Tenochtitlán's center. Temples, shrines to the gods, were built on the truncated pyramid peaks. Castles to house the rich were erected near the pyramids. Some of the castles had fifty or more rooms. A huge public square and marketplace sprawled in front of the city's tallest pyramid. Canals boats carried goods to the market. Beholding this wonderful city, an Aztec poet wrote:

> The city is spread out in circles of jade
> Radiating flashes of light . . .
> Beside it the lords are borne in boats:
> Over them extends a flowery mist.

The army remained the Aztec nation's strongest institution. Every boy in Aztec society was first and foremost a soldier. Military duty for boys began at infancy. The midwife, who assisted the mother at birth, was required to place a toy bow or spear in every baby boy's hand and say a special prayer: "My very loved and tender son, here is the doctrine that was given to us by the gods. This place where you were born is not your true house, because you are a soldier . . . You are promised to the field of battle."

Starting at the age of six, boys from working-class families attended boarding schools where they were taught the art of spear throwing and fighting with a club. Rules were strict. A boy who violated the rules in any manner was expected to punish himself by sticking a cactus thorn through his tongue or his earlobe. Upper-class boys went to an even harsher school called the calmecac (House of Pain), where students slept on bare brick floors and were forced to bathe in icy waters. Teenagers joined the regular army and soon experienced battle. Success on the battlefield was the only way a young man could advance in Aztec society.

Fearlessness was the rule in the Aztec army. Any display of cowardice called for the death penalty, but rarely did that penalty have to be imposed. Soldiers believed their lives belonged to their nation and to their gods. In fact, death itself was accepted in Aztec society as something inevitable and natural, like the changing of the seasons. The transitory nature of life can be seen in a favorite Aztec poem:

> We only came to sleep
> we only came to dream
> it is not true, no it is not true
> that we came to live on earth.

Steadily the Aztec nation grew through military conquest. Step by step and battle by battle, the Aztec army conquered the Valley of Mexico. The tribes that once scorned the outsiders from the northern desert now accepted Aztec rule, often without a fight. When the Aztec army approached a rival city, their soldiers staged elaborate prebattle rituals. Men in ranks performed wild war dances and musicians blew conch horns and shrill whistles made from bones. Just the sight of this fierce army was enough to force a city's surrender.

From the Valley of Mexico, Aztec influence spread in every direction. By the early 1500s the Aztecs controlled an empire which stretched more than 100,000 square miles. The empire ran from the Atlantic to the Pacific and embraced

12 million people. This territory was not a kingdom in the European sense where all subjects lived under one central government. Instead it was a collection of vassal cities and states that were required to pay taxes and tributes to the Aztec ruler. Tributes included gold, silver, precious feathers, and finely woven cloth. Treasures flowing in as tribute made Tenochtitlán beyond comparison the richest city in Mexico. Tributes also included men and women to be sacrificed on Aztec altars.

Pleasing the gods was the primary mission of the Aztec nation. The Aztecs worshipped hundreds of gods including a god of rain, a god of fire, and a god of the winds. Special gods ruled over each division of the day: the morning, the afternoon, and the evening. Merchants prayed to merchant gods for aid in the sale of their goods. Soldiers paid homage to military gods and asked their graces to provide victories on the battlefield.

Rising above all other gods in the Aztec pantheon was Huitzilopochtli, the Hummingbird. When the Aztecs were wanderers, the Hummingbird was their god of the hunt. As a military nation, Huitzilopochtli climbed in status to become the god of war. By the time the Aztecs were a great society, the Hummingbird ruled over all life on earth. Without the Hummingbird's blessings the world was doomed. And Huitzilopochtli—as was true with most of the other gods—demanded the hearts of men and women.

The killing of human beings as part of religious ritual was practiced by most ancient societies, but no other culture took the custom to the grisly heights of the Aztecs. Early in Aztec history, human sacrifice was an occasional act in religious ceremonies. Then, starting in 1450, frosts and droughts destroyed crops for four straight years. So many people died of starvation that Aztec society faced eradication.

Priests claimed the gods were angry at the Aztecs and sent the drought to destroy their crops. Those gods demanded human blood in order to soothe their anger. Aztec armies launched a series of invasions and captured thousands of prisoners, all of whom were sacrificed to the gods. Oddly the magic worked. Rains came and crops grew again. The Aztecs never forgot what they perceived as the benefits of human sacrifice. As the nation's power increased so did the appetites of their gods.

The most common method of the Aztec human sacrifice was to lead victims to the altar of a temple. There the victim was placed face up on a sacrificial stone. Four priests held the person down while another priest cut open his chest. The priest then reached into the cavity and took out the heart while it was still beating. The heart was held triumphantly before the statue of the god, and the victim's blood was sprinkled on the temple floor. In Tenochtitlán this gory procedure was carried out in front of thousands of onlookers. The beating of a giant snakeskin drum perched high on a wall drowned out the victim's screams.

The flesh of the victim was eaten by nobles and high-ranking army officers. The practice of cannibalism also grew as the Aztec nation expanded and the gods increased their demands. By eating human flesh it was believed that the living absorbed the spirit and the power of the dead. Only leaders in Aztec society were allowed to eat human flesh, and some of them considered it to be a delicacy. Written recipes told cooks how to make stews out of cornmeal and human meat with chili peppers as a spice.

Sacrificial victims were often prisoners of war. Aztec soldiers were taught to capture enemy warriors. Those who successfully took prisoners on the battlefield were given special feathers to wear during military parades. Killing a foe in battle was regarded as careless and inconsiderate because it robbed the gods of their food. The hearts of brave soldiers were most desirable, as they gave the deities strength. Often the Aztecs fought prearranged "flower wars" with other nations for the purpose of gaining captives.

Victims were treated with dignity up to the final, awful moment of their lives. Human sacrifice was widespread in Mexico, and most victims believed that death on an altar would usher them into a heavenly world where they would be a "companion of the eagle." A soldier who captured another man in battle commonly led the captive to the altar and said a prayer, "Here is my well-beloved son." The captive then replied, "Here is my revered father."

Aztec priests were not above sacrificing their own people. Slaves and men who had fallen into debt were offered to the gods. Women were sacrificed, but not as frequently as were men. Even children were sometimes put to death at the altars. Tlaloc, the rain god, desired the lives of children. The amount of tears the children and their parents shed before their deaths determined the amount of rain Tlaloc would grant to Aztec farmers.

Historians today argue over the number of people killed each year in Aztec temples. Many historians claim that the Spaniards later exaggerated that number in order to brand the Aztecs as a devilish people and therefore justify their conquest and enslavement.

The Races of Mexico

Mexico is a multiracial society, and the issue of race is also complex. The vast majority of people in Mexico are *mestizos*, meaning mixed race. But the country is also home to *indios*, (Indians, the indigenous people of Mexico), *negros*, (blacks, tens of thousands of whom were brought by the Spanish as slaves), and whites. White is generally used to describe Spaniards, and any non-Spanish whites are generally labeled by nationality rather than race: American, German, British, etc.

Despite some exaggerated accounts, there is no doubt that human sacrifice was central to Aztec religious worship. Aztec records claim as many as 20,000 victims met their deaths when a newly built pyramid to Huitzilopochtli was dedicated in 1487. During that bloody ceremony, the lines of victims stretched three miles long and exhausted priests worked in relays tearing out hearts. The entire city stank like a slaughterhouse for weeks after the massacre.

The Aztecs saw war everywhere—in the heavens, under the earth, and within the souls of men and women. The sun did not simply rise in the morning. Instead the gods of light fought the forces of darkness. Inside the bodies of people the angels of good health battled the devils of sickness. Warfare was constant and universal. The gods who blessed the nation required human hearts in order to triumph over evil spirits. Death at the altars was neither a happy nor a sad event. It was the way of the universe, the way things must be done.

THREE

God, Gold, and Glory

F our thousand miles from the land of the Aztecs lay the kingdom of Spain. It too was a god-fearing militaristic society. For seven hundred years the Spaniards fought the Moors who came up from Africa and occupied most of their country. The Moors were Muslim; the Spaniards Christian. Warfare between the two peoples took on a religious passion. When not fighting the Moors, the Spaniards fought each other. Spain was a tangle of fiercely independent provinces which engaged in regular civil wars.

In the late 1400s the political situation in Spain began to stabilize. A marriage between Princess Isabella of the province of Castile and Prince Ferdinand of Aragon gave Spain unity and put an end to the civil wars. In 1492 Spanish soldiers drove the Moors out of the city of Granada, their last bastion in the country. The Granada victory was described by a Spanish official as, "the most distinguished and blessed day that there ever had been in Spain."

Contemporary photograph of Granada

Now unified and free from foreign rule, Spain stood ready to become a world power. Yet the culture of war prevailed in the minds of the people. Soldiering was an honored and heroic profession in the Spanish mind. Manly courage was the accepted standard for all Spaniards. Any display of cowardice in battle or in one's personal life was an unthinkable disgrace.

The new Spanish state emerged at the beginning of an era of exploration which saw Europeans search the seas for new and strange lands. Profit motivated the exploration urge. Silk and spices from Asia brought high prices in European markets. But a trading mission to Asia was long and arduous as merchants had to traverse both land and sea. Some merchants entertained the idea of reaching the eastern ports by sailing

Christopher Columbus

west. Educated Europeans believed the world was spherical. Therefore a ship ought to be able to sail to China and the spice-rich islands called the Indies by circling the globe.

A leading exponent of a westward voyage to the Orient was the Italian navigator Christopher Columbus. He met with Queen Isabella of Spain hoping she would finance a voyage to the east. Isabella was Catholic and wanted to win new souls for Christ. At first the Queen's advisors urged her not to finance Columbus' enterprise because such a voyage had never been tried before. Isabella remained interested and Columbus was persistent. Columbus finally secured Spain's backing and set sail with three ships in August of 1492.

For more than thirty days Columbus led the fleet westward and could find no sign of land. This was a terrifying experience for the men. Sea captains of the time tried to plot their courses so their vessels hugged the shorelines and crews rarely lost sight of land. Now, surrounded by nothing but endless waves, the sailors believed they were doomed. Finally, on the thirty-third day, a lookout shouted, "Land! Land!" Columbus and his three tiny ships completed the most famous voyage of discovery in world history.

The ships had reached the Caribbean Sea near the American continent. Columbus believed these islands were the Indies, where delicious spices grow. He called the natives he met Indians, a mistaken term that persists to this day. The Europeans probed the waters and sailed around the large island of Cuba, which they thought was Japan. The Spaniards under Columbus set up a headquarters on the smaller island they called Hispaniola (today's Haiti and the Dominican Republic).

A fifteenth century map of Hispaniola

The *Fountain of Youth*, portrayed here by Dutch artist Lucas Cranach, was believed to be located in the Americas.

Christopher Columbus made two more voyages to the Americas. He died in 1506, still thinking the Caribbean islands he had found were the Indies and the gateway to fortunes in trade. At his death he was deeply in debt and disgraced because his voyages had brought no profits in trade to the Spanish crown.

The discoveries of Columbus excited the men of Spain. For years Spain was haunted by stories of fabulous civilizations that lie somewhere across the waters. One writer of adventure stories told of a lush and beautiful island called California. Other fanciful tales said that somewhere to the west was a magical fountain whose waters had the ability to restore youth to the old and feeble.

All Europeans puzzled over a strange letter to the Catholic Pope which appeared about 1160. The letter was from a certain Prester John who claimed to be the Christian leader of a country in the Orient. Tales said John's distant nation possessed a magical mirror which allowed its leader to peer into every province of his domain. Today historians believe the original Prester John letter was a very clever forgery. Who committed the forgery and the motives behind it are mysteries.

Gold held a special power over the Spaniards. Not only did gold provide comforts on earth, but a person could contribute gold to the Church and buy a particularly happy place in heaven. The adventure writers told stories of cities in the Orient whose streets were paved with gold tiles.

Religious zeal also drove young Spaniards to dream about crossing the ocean. The Spaniards believed they were soldiers of Christ and that it was their duty to spread the word of the true faith to all people. Converting nonbelievers to Christianity was another method that would usher a man into heaven upon his death.

The men of Spain who descended on the Americas after the voyage of Columbus were called conquistadors, conquerors. They were armed with superior weapons and driven by religious zeal as well as greed. Historians have since summed up their mission in the New World in three words: God, gold, and glory.

The greatest of all conquistadors was Hernando Cortés, born in 1485. Cortés grew up in the dry and barren province of Extremadura which lies near Spain's border with Portugal. Treeless and windswept, Extremadura was a land of sheep farms and—most important—a nurturing place for soldiers.

Hernando Cortés

With no practical way to make a living the youth of Extremadura turned to the military. Extremadurans earned the reputation as the fiercest fighters in Spain, a kingdom of warriors.

The Cortés family held the rank of minor nobility. The father was an officer in the cavalry, and the mother a sternly religious Catholic. Francisco López de Gómara worked as Cortés's secretary and later wrote his biography, *Cortés: The Life of the Conqueror by his Secretary.* Gómara said of the Cortés family, "They had little wealth but much honor, a thing that rarely occurs except among those of virtuous life."

When Cortés was fourteen, his parents sent him to the city of Salamanca to study Latin and the law. He was probably an excellent student, because he later displayed an extraordinary skill in the Latin language. In those days Latin was the language of the Catholic Church and of the intellectuals. But young Cortés leaned more towards adventure than study. He stayed at the university in Salamanca for only two years. Gómara said of Cortés at this period of his life, "He was a source of trouble to his parents as well as to himself, for he was restless, haughty, mischievous, and given to quarreling."

Cortés was an avid reader of adventure stories. He believed a fortune awaited the young and the brave. A plan worked through his mind. He would board a ship and journey to the lands called the Indies. His parents helped him raise money to pay for the voyage. Gómara said, "Cortés was nineteen when he went to the Indies in the year of Our Lord 1504."

A journey across the Atlantic usually took two months, and it was dangerous and woefully uncomfortable. Cortés was jammed into a ship with scores of other Spanish adventure-seekers. The men tried to sleep on deck but rains often drove them below, where they had to find space in a cargo hold crawling with rats. On Cortés's ship the drinking water turned green after a few weeks at sea, and worms infested the bread. Worse yet, the ship was lashed by a violent Atlantic storm. The men aboard were certain they would be swallowed up by mountainous waves which tossed their vessel about as if it were a toy. Gómara reported, "The sailors were filled with anxiety . . . and the passengers wept . . . All [made confessions]; some cursed their luck; others awaited death."

Miraculously the ship survived and Cortés and his fellow Spaniards landed on the island of Hispaniola. Like Cortés, most of the soldiers came from families which held noble titles but had little wealth. Arrogant and proud, these young aristocrats refused to perform practical work such as farming and fishing. Instead they enslaved the natives and forced them to tend to their needs.

There were few Spanish women in the early camps, and this was unfortunate. Perhaps the presence of women would have civilized the behavior of the youthful noblemen. Reeking with feelings of superiority, the men launched a reign of terror in the Caribbean.

The island of Hispaniola was home to a simple people, called the Tainos. They raised sweet potatoes and corn, fished, and made pottery. Their climate was pleasant and the land and the sea gave them all they needed or desired. One Spanish official said, "Amongst them the land belongs to everyone, just as does the sun and the water . . . they live in gardens open to all, without laws and without judges."

At first the Tainos worshipped the white-skinned strangers as if they were gods. The Spaniards looked down upon them as heathens who knew nothing of Christ. And the Tainos had little gold. This lack of gold enraged the Europeans. Wantonly the Spaniards murdered the Taino men and raped the women. A Spanish priest named Bartolomé de las Casas wrote a desperate letter to the King, "They [the Spaniards] make bets on who among them could slice a man in half, or decapitate him or gut him with a single sword-stroke . . . They took infants from their mothers' breasts, swung them by the legs and shattered their heads against boulders."

From Hispaniola, the Spanish reign of terror spread to neighboring islands. The conquistadors captured Puerto Rico in 1508 and Jamaica in 1509. By this time the Europeans were less concerned as to whether these islands were the Indies of lore, as Columbus believed. The invaders now simply wished to exploit the lands and the people and reap profits.

The Spaniards established plantations and forced the natives to work as slaves in sugarcane fields. Indian slave labor was also used to mine the little gold that could be found in the islands. Because they felt it was their duty, the Spaniards introduced the Christian Bible to the islanders. If, in the opinion of their Spanish masters, the people failed to obey the Commandments they were tortured and killed.

Spanish rule devastated the Caribbean region. Native men committed suicide and women aborted their babies, acts

Illustrations of acts the Spanish committed against the Indians

that were almost unheard of in these lands before Columbus. Spaniards brought European cattle and pigs to the islands. The livestock roamed freely, ruining native farms. Rats, previously unknown on the islands, climbed off Spanish ships and ravaged crops.

Overwork, poor food, and disease took a heavy toll of lives. As many as 200,000 Tainos lived on Hispaniola in 1492; a little more than ten years later the population was reduced to about 30,000.

Hernando Cortés stayed on Hispaniola for seven years. He built a business as a trader and served as an official in the small Spanish settlement called Azúa. Cortés acquired several Taino slaves, and according to reports he was kind to them in stark contrast to his fellow Spaniards. When not attending to business he gambled and fought duels with other Spaniards over the right to court the few Spanish women on Hispaniola. Sword fighting left him with several facial cuts, but in the Spanish colonies such dueling scars were considered the mark of a man.

In 1511, when he was twenty-six, Cortés participated in an invasion of Cuba. The large island of Cuba was home to a people called the Caribs (the word Caribbean Sea is derived from their name). The Caribs fought the invaders, but had little chance against well-armed and superbly disciplined Spanish soldiers. Cortés saw his first real combat on Cuba, and he fought bravely.

As masters of Cuba, the Spaniards imposed their customary harsh rule on the people. The measure of Spanish cruelty can be seen in the story of Hatuey, a chieftain who escaped from Hispaniola and fled to Cuba. Hatuey was convicted of rebellion against the Spanish king and sentenced to death. A priest urged him to accept baptism so he might go to heaven and escape the fires of hell. Hatuey asked if there were Spaniards in this place called heaven; the priest said indeed there were. Hatuey refused to be baptized. He claimed he did not want to go anywhere—including to a paradise—if there was even one Spaniard there.

Cortés was given a ranch on Cuba where he raised cattle and sheep. He also owned several gold mines. Of his mining ventures, Gómara said, "[Cortés] extracted a great deal of gold with the labor of his Indians and soon was rich . . ."

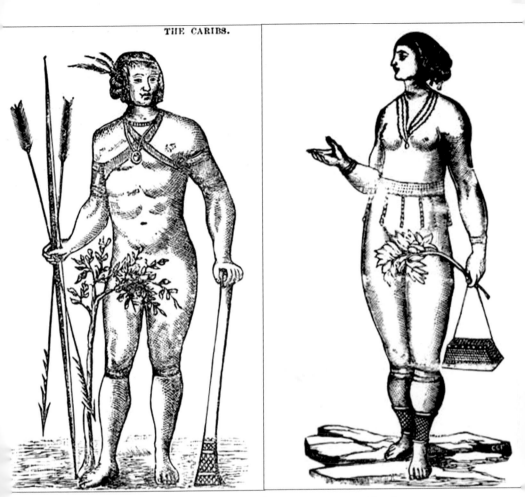

The Carib people lived in Cuba until they were conquered by the Spanish. *(Library of Congress)*

In 1515 Cortés married a Spanish woman named Catalina. The couple quarreled frequently, but using Cortés's money they built one of the finest houses anywhere in the New World. By all measures he was a successful man. But he had not crossed the sea to be a rancher or a gold miner. Somewhere in these new lands was a rich civilization which he could discover and conquer. There he would tell the people of the true faith. This was his mission, his destiny—God, gold, glory!

The conquered Caribs told the Spaniards that there were lands to the north and west of their islands. The Spaniards believed these lands, if they existed, were other islands. There still was no understanding by Spaniards in the Caribbean that the huge American continent was their next-door neighbor.

In 1517 three Spanish ships, commanded by Francisco de Córdoba, left Cuba and sailed on a westerly course. After several days at sea the sailors spotted land. Venturing closer, the men saw what appeared to be a great city with pyramids rising from the mists. This was astonishing. Nowhere thus far in the New World had Spaniards beheld stone buildings. Two large Indian canoes came toward the ships and the men aboard beckoned as if welcoming the Spaniards. The Spaniards launched two of their own small boats and the crews rowed ashore. All seemed peaceful.

Then, on the beach, the Spaniards were bombarded by a rain of arrows. They had walked into an ambush. Shrieking Indians charged at them from all sides. But in close battle Spanish steel swords and armor prevailed. European firearms, clumsy weapons called arquebuses, terrified the Indians. It was the first time the natives had seen such devices that spat out thunder and lightning. The Indians fled, leaving more than a dozen of their warriors dead on the beach.

Marching inland, the Spaniards entered the city they had seen from the sea. It was deserted. The residents abandoned their homes at the sound of the battle. Overwhelmed, the Spaniards marveled at their surroundings. The men of Spain commented to each other that these buildings were as substantial as any that could be found in their native country.

Slowly the city dwellers drifted back to their homes. Friendly gestures prevailed. The Spaniards were fed. Goods such as trinkets and beads were traded between the two peoples. To the great delight of the Spaniards, these people even had small objects made from gold and silver.

The Córdoba expedition had reached what is now the state of Yucatán on Mexico's southeastern coast. The pyramids and stone cities that had so dazzled them were built by the Mayas. Though the Maya civilization was in decline, its cities were still formidable and deeply impressed the Spaniards.

Córdoba next sailed along the Yucatán coast until he spotted another city. Once more the men went ashore and once more they were attacked. This time the battle was a disaster for the Spaniards. Hundreds of Maya warriors, swinging wooden clubs with sharp obsidian stone blades at their tips, swarmed upon the small Spanish force. As one soldier wrote, "[They] attacked us hand to hand, some with lances, and the others shooting arrows, and others with two-handed knife edge swords."

The Spaniards retreated to their ships after suffering many deaths and injuries. The Maya, the Spaniards learned, were aggressive and brave fighters. Captain Córdoba was badly hurt in the battle and later died of his wounds.

The Remarkable Mayas

The Mayas reached their peak in about 200 to 800 AD. Their nation spread over southern Mexico and into Central America. They were one of the most brilliant civilizations in the Americas. Mayan art and architecture was among the most advanced in the entire ancient world. Mayan mathematicians achieved the concept of absolute zero centuries ahead of the Europeans.

Despite the dangers, the Maya cities discovered by Cordoba intrigued the Spaniards in Cuba. In May 1518 a fleet under the command of Juan de Grijalva set out for the Yucatán coast. The Spaniards fought several skirmishes with the Mayas.

But Juan de Grijalva was more eager to talk and trade goods than to make war. Eventually he did talk to the Maya leaders, as best as he could through sign language and gestures. The Mayas brought the Spaniards gifts, including many well-crafted gold statues. Captain Grijalva asked where he could obtain still more gold. The Mayas pointed westward toward the mountains and said, "*México, México.*"

Coastal people called the Aztecs the Mexica, and their great capital city was known as Mexico.

FOUR

The Lure of Mexico

In the Aztec capital Emperor Montezuma (also spelled Moctezuma) had every reason to believe he was the most powerful man on earth. His empire ranged from ocean to ocean and his armies were invincible. The Aztec capital city, an island fortress, had never even been attacked by an enemy army. Contemplating this mighty city, an Aztec poet asked: "Who could conquer Tenochtitlán? / Who could shake the foundation of heaven . . .?"

Yet Montezuma was troubled. He became emperor in 1502. His grandfather was one of the wisest and greatest kings in Aztec history. In his youth Montezuma was an army commander, brilliant on the battlefield. As emperor he was expected to be a religious leader, and in this capacity he was less sure of his abilities. There were so many gods whose messages he had to hear. So many signs in the stars and elsewhere had to be read in order to plot a proper future for his nation. And the signs he saw about him were disturbing.

The Aztec Emperor Montezuma

A comet with three heads, described as a "flaming ear of corn," hung over the Aztec capital for months. Lightning struck a temple on the city's highest pyramid and the temple burned to ashes despite the efforts of crews to douse the blaze. Men armed with swords were said to be seen fighting in the sky. At night Tenochtitlán residents claimed they

A comet sighted over Tenochtitlan was viewed as an omen.

heard the chilling voice of a weeping woman who cried out
in anguish: "O my beloved sons, we are all going to die. My
beloved sons, where shall I hide you?"

In the Aztec mind the gods were at work everywhere. To
keep the gods satisfied the practice of human sacrifice had
to be continued and even increased in times of peril. But not
all the gods demanded human hearts.

La Llorona

The weeping woman tale continued in Mexico for centuries
as a scary story told by children. Kids would try to frighten
each other by saying the woman, La Llorona, lost her children
and now she was coming to get YOU. Every village had its own
Llorona and the favorite places she liked to haunt. Today TV and
the Internet have taken the fright out of the tale and La Llorona
is remembered mainly by grandparents.

Aztec god Quetzalcóatl

One powerful god, Quetzalcóatl (kehts-uhl-KUH-wah-tl), was a rebel. Quetzalcóatl, the feathered serpent, was the god of air, water, and the ripples made by wind as it flows over a calm lake. It was said the god once lived with various tribes in Mexico, including with the Toltec people. He taught the Toltecs metalworking and showed them new farming techniques. He, alone among the gods, condemned human sacrifice. Quetzalcóatl preferred gifts of flowers and butterflies rather than bloody human hearts.

Centuries ago, according to legends, a rival god rose up and drove Quetzalcóatl out of Mexico. He was last seen riding on the back of a feathered serpent which flew above the waters of the Atlantic Ocean. He flew east and disappeared over the endless sea. Before his flight, the god vowed to return some day and claim all of Mexico as his own.

Aztec calendar

Montezuma now pondered reports from the Maya lands to the south that strange white men were seen along the coast riding in vessels with clouds above them. In ancient pictures Quetzalcóatl was always drawn as a white man with a beard. Writings said Quetzalcóatl gave a date for his return: He would come back in the year One Reed on the Aztec calendar; that year on the European calendar was 1519.

Diego Velázquez, the governor of Cuba, initially backed Cortés's expedition.

In Cuba, in early 1519, the Spaniards prepared to send another mission westward toward Mexico. The Spanish governor of Cuba was a fat, jolly man named Diego Velázquez. He had first come to the New World with Columbus. He acted as a father figure for the young conquistadors, and one of his best friends was Hernando Cortés. Velázquez admired Cortés's intelligence and his courage. However the governor was wary of the young man's burning ambition. Cortés was a rising star, an aggressive person who wanted to be the richest and most powerful Spaniard in the New World. Spanish soldiers were madly jealous of each other's status. All men of Spain sought power.

Exploration missions in the New World were privately financed. Velázquez had paid for the voyages of both

Francisco Hernández Córdoba and Diego Velazquez from his own pocket. By law he was obliged to pay one-fifth of any gold or profits reaped by the voyages to the Spanish crown. He was willing to pay this Quintero or "King's Fifth," as no Spaniard would dream of cheating the monarch out of his taxes.

The voyage Velázquez planned would be the largest and most expensive one yet, and he hoped to have other backers to help pay the costs. Cortés, with his cattle ranches and gold mines, was one of the wealthiest men in Cuba. The governor met with Cortés and the two agreed to finance the venture jointly. They also agreed that Cortés would command the mission.

Velázquez soon regretted his choice of a partner. He feared the ambitious Cortés would try to set up his own private empire in this land called Mexico. As Cortés gathered ships and men, the governor wrote an order forbidding the fleet to sail. But Cortés had spies on the governor's staff. He readied his ships, chose his soldiers, and set sail before the written order could be delivered to him. Furious, Governor Velázquez swore he would punish the insolent Cortés.

On February 19, 1519, Hernando Cortés sailed away from Cuba. He was thirty-three years old and had spent seven years on Hispaniola and seven years on Cuba. His fleet consisted of eleven ships. Aboard were one hundred sailors, 550 soldiers, sixteen horses, ten brass guns, and four small cannons. This tiny force would soon confront an empire whose leaders commanded many thousands of warriors.

Before setting out, Cortés gave his men an inspirational speech, recorded by López de Gómora. Cortés predicted—accurately, it turned out—that this mission to Mexico would make history:

> Certain it is, my friends and companions, that every good man of spirit strives, by his own effort, to make himself the equal of the excellent men of his day and even of the past. And so it is that I am embarking on a great and beautiful enterprise, which will be famous in times to come, because I know in my heart that we shall take vast and wealthy lands, people such as have never been seen, and kingdoms greater than those of our monarchs.

First to arrive in Mexican waters was a lone ship commanded by Pedro de Alvarado, one of Cortés's highest lieutenants. A big, red-headed man, Alvarado was known for his fiery temper. His ship approached Cozumel Island which at the time held about 3,000 people who made their living by fishing. Most of the residents raced into the woods at the sight of the Spanish vessel.

Pedro de Alvarado was one of Cortés's high-ranking officers, but his temper and proclivity towards violence frequently caused trouble.

The Spaniards landed, looted a fishing village, and took three Indians prisoner. In the houses they found very little gold. Alvarado suspected a treasure in gold was somewhere nearby. He demanded to know where the gold was hidden and threatened to torture his captives. Just then Captain Hernando Cortés appeared.

Cortés was furious with Alvarado. He hoped to negotiate with the people of Mexico and fight them only when necessary. Cortés needed friends and allies in these lands. According to one soldier, "[Cortés] reprimanded Pedro de Alvarado severely, and told him we should never pacify the country in that way by robbing the natives of their property."

Cortés ordered the prisoners to be released and all stolen goods returned immediately. Fellow conquistadors were shocked by what seemed to be an act of compassion from their leader. Cruelty and war were the rule when taking and plundering the Caribbean Islands. Here Captain Cortés was at least willing to try a different policy.

Cozumel Today

Cozumel is Mexico's largest island. Today it is a seaside resort famed for its beautiful reefs where vacationers enjoy scuba diving and snorkeling.

As they made ready to leave Cozumel the Spaniards saw a canoe in the waters bearing a nearly naked man. Paddling nearer, the man surprised the Cortés soldiers by saying, in perfect Spanish, "Gentlemen, are you Christians?"

The stranger was Gerónimo de Aguilar, a Spaniard who had come to the Caribbean ten years earlier. He had a wild and chilling story to tell. In 1511 he was on a routine voyage when his ship struck rocks near the island of Jamaica and sank. About twenty survivors saved themselves by boarding lifeboats. The boats were swept by ferocious winds and currents to the Yucatán coast. Half of those on board died before reaching shore. The others were captured by Maya warriors. One by one they were sacrificed on Maya altars and their flesh eaten. The Mayas practiced human sacrifice, although not on the large scale of the Aztecs.

Two men, Aguilar and one Gonzalo Guerrero, were spared immediate sacrifice. They were put in cages and fed in order to fatten them up so they could be sacrificed and eaten at a coming festival. Both men escaped and fled to a neighboring village where they were kept as slaves.

Aguilar claimed that constant prayer and faith in God kept him alive and sane during this ordeal. The other man, Guerrero, survived by assimilating into the native culture. He worshipped Maya gods and tattooed his face and neck, as was the custom among coastal people. Guerrero married a Maya girl and now headed a family with three children. He claimed he did not ever wish to join Spanish society again. In fact, Guerrero was at this time warning the Maya people that Spaniards were evil men who would steal their goods and kill them.

Cortés allowed Gerónimo de Aguilar to join his expedition. Meeting this captive of the Maya was a stroke of luck for his mission. Aguilar was fluent in the Maya language. He also spoke Spanish, though his native tongue was rusty after nine years in captivity. Aguilar served as a valuable interpreter for Cortés.

Next the ships probed the southern coast of Mexico, sailing along shore to find a good place to drop anchor. Some of the men took a small boat and went fishing. They had no idea they were being watched by Aztec agents. One agent spotted the Spanish ships and hurried the great distances over the mountains to tell Montezuma: "Our lord and king, it is true that strange people have come to the shores of the great sea. They were fishing from a small boat, some with rods and others with a net . . . then they got into a canoe and went back to their two great towers [meaning a ship with two tall masts], and climbed up into them. They have very light skin, much lighter than ours."

Bearded white men, as pictured in the ancient drawings of Quetzalcóatl, had appeared. They arrived on the eastern shores, precisely where Quetzalcóatl had left Mexico centuries ago riding on a winged serpent. And the white men came in the year One Reed, the same year the legends claimed the god swore to return. Montezuma, a mortal man, believed he was about to face a god.

The Cortés expedition first touched the beach on mainland Mexico near the present day city of Campeche. This spot was visited by both previous Spanish voyages, and waiting at the beach was an old friend. A dog, described by Gómara as a, "large greyhound . . . came up to them wagging her tail, running from one to the other, barking and jumping up on them with her forepaws." No such large dogs were native to Mexico, and the men concluded the greyhound was accidentally left behind by one of the other Spanish missions. The dog apparently did quite well by eating rabbits. Now she happily joined the Cortés army.

In late March the Spaniards came ashore to get water at the mouth of the Tabasco River. They were promptly attacked by Tabascan warriors. Thousands of painted Indians fired arrows and threw rocks at the Spanish ranks. Shrieking

St. James (Santiago) was a disciple of Jesus. Spanish lore claims he miraculously reappeared in the fifteenth century and helped the Spanish defeat the Moors, inspiring this portrait and the battle cry of "Santiago y a ellos!"

war whoops, the Tabascans charged the vastly outnumbered Spaniards. It was here that Cortés first shouted the Spanish war cry which would become familiar in Mexico: "Santiago y a ellos" (Saint James and at them). The soldiers responded to this command by chanting Santiago! Santiago!

The men of Spain stood in tight ranks, back-to-back. Forming a square, they fended off Tabascan attacks with spears and swords. The enemy too fought bravely. Spanish artillery thundered and killed and wounded hundreds of Tabascans. Still they pressed forward.

Finally Cortés brought his ultimate weapon to the battle. From the trees to the rear galloped the few horsemen on the Cortés mission. The people of Mexico had never seen a horse before. This was a godlike animal. The Tabascans believed the horse and rider were one and the same being. At one point a Spanish horseman fell off his mount, and then jumped back into the saddle. The action froze the Tabascans with terror. This creature could split apart and then rejoin itself at will. The battle ended in an overwhelming Spanish victory.

The next day, after the dust of battle settled, Cortés made peace with the Tabascan chief. He allowed the Tabascans to bury their dead, as was their custom. The chief gave the Spaniards gifts, including gold ornaments and twenty women slaves. Among the slaves was a beautiful teenager who carried herself with the grace and dignity of a princess. A priest baptized the women, since Cortés forbade any of his men to sleep with heathens. After baptism the women were distributed to the men to serve as mistresses. Spaniards called the

Malinche helped translate for Cortés, making her essential to the success of the Spanish army.

beautiful teenager Doña Marina. Her fellow Indians called her Malinche. She became Cortés's mistress and made herself indispensable to the army commander. In the future the young Malinche rose to become a towering figure in Mexican history.

The Spanish fleet followed the Mexican coast. On April 21, 1519, the ships dropped anchor at an island in a fine natural harbor. The harbor itself became Veracruz, the first permanent Spanish settlement in Mexico.

Almost immediately after landing the Spaniards were greeted by dignitaries who were envoys of Emperor Montezuma. The Aztec chief had followed the Spaniards' activities closely through agents and spies. He knew about the incredible battle that took place along the Tabascan River and how a handful of these foreigners defeated thousands of Indian warriors. Upon seeing Cortés the Aztecs representatives lay prostate before him and uttered the words Montezuma had instructed them to say, "Hear us, o god, your vassal Montezuma bids you welcome."

Talking to the Aztec representatives established the value of the slave girl Malinche. She had been born into a noble family in the Aztec lands. After the death of her father she was sold as a slave to the Maya peoples. Consequently she spoke Nahuatl, the language of the Aztecs, and she spoke the Maya dialect which was understood by the shipwrecked Spaniard, Aguilar. During discussions she took the Aztec words and translated them into Maya, which Aguilar in turn translated into Spanish. The process required a complicated three-way conversation, but it worked. Cortés had a team of excellent translators.

Coldly, Cortés spoke with the Aztec dignitaries. When the Spanish leader wished to put on airs, he could be a splendid actor. He accepted the gifts the Aztecs presented: finely woven robes, jewelry, small statues made of gold. All these gifts were lovely, he said, but he wanted more. He demanded to go to the Aztec capital and speak directly with Emperor Montezuma.

The Aztec representatives were shocked. They claimed they could not authorize such a meeting. An angry Cortés ordered the Aztecs to be chained. He then put on a dazzling display of military might and required them to watch. His horse soldiers pranced their steeds along the beach, making sure the animals neighed and snorted. Huge Spanish war dogs, fierce Irish wolfhounds, were taken on leashes and made to growl and snarl at the terrified Aztecs. The Spaniards fired their cannon with an earsplitting roar, the ball shattering a tree.

Finally Cortés released Montezuma's ambassadors and ordered them to return home and tell their chief what they had seen. As a final gesture he gave them a soldier's helmet and commanded they return it filled with gold. He said, "I and my companions suffer from a disease of the heart which can be cured only by gold."

The shaken ambassadors hurried the two-hundred-fifty miles back to Tenochtitlán. They hardly paused to rest. In the capital they reported to Montezuma that the foreigners have a weapon of thunder and fire. "A thing like a ball of stones comes out of its entrails: it comes out shooting sparks and raining fire . . . If it is aimed against a tree, it shatters the tree into splinters . . . Their deer [horses] carry them on their backs wherever they wish to go. These deer, our lord, are as tall as the roof of a house . . . Their dogs are enormous, with flat ears and long, dangling tongues."

The ambassadors said their leader was a white man with a thick black beard, just like the ancient pictures of Quetzalcóatl. They came exactly when and where the legends said Quetzalcóatl would return. They were invincible in battle and they possessed magical weapons. Montezuma wondered: were they not divine creatures led by a god?

The people of the Veracruz region were called the Totonacs. Through their talk Cortés learned they were bitter enemies of the Aztecs. Cortés asked to see the Totonac chief. He was told the chief was too fat to travel, but he would be glad to greet the Spaniards in his capital city which was a few miles away. In those days being overweight was a sign of prosperity, and the Spaniards determined the Totonacs must be a rich people.

Cortés and his men marched to the Totonac capital. There they were presented to the chief, who was indeed hefty. The Spaniards nicknamed him the "fat cacique." Cacique was a Caribbean word for leader, and the Spaniards applied it to every chief they met in Mexico. The fat cacique complained to Cortés that the Aztecs forced his people to send high tributes to Tenochtitlán. They were obliged to pay gold, cloth, precious stones, and to give slaves who were sacrificed on Aztec altars.

Just as they were talking five Aztec tax collectors entered the city, seeking a payment of slaves. Cortés ordered his men to seize the Aztecs and chain them to a tree. The fat cacique was startled that anyone would treat the powerful Aztecs in such a crude manner. Later that night Cortés secretly freed the tax collectors, and told them he was doing this in order to prove to Montezuma he was a friend of the Aztecs.

Every morning the Spaniards stayed with the Totonacs three or four people were taken up the steps of the city's main pyramid and sacrificed. The blood and stink of this process disgusted the Spaniards, and it violated their religious principals. Cortés had already determined to use the Totonacs as allies in a planned march on the Aztecs. But first these heathens had to learn something of Christianity.

Cortés ordered fifty of his men to climb the high pyramid, tear down the idol that stood in the temple at the peak, and replace it with a cross. He announced through his interpreters that from now on human sacrifice was forbidden. The Totonacs were stunned at this audacious act. One Spaniard wrote, "When the chiefs and the people saw their idols broken and lying on the ground they set up a miserable howl, covered their faces, and begged forgiveness of the idols that they were unable to protect them."

Point of View

In journal after journal Spaniards wrote about the shock and horror they felt when observing human sacrifice as performed in Mexico. Many Spaniards argued that human sacrifice proved the Mexicans were inferior to Europeans and therefore it was justified to conquer and enslave them. But the Spaniards practiced their own violent and terrible religious rites, and they too believed they were acting in the name of God. The conquistadors lived in Spain during the Inquisition, a time of religious fanaticism when those suspected of being unfaithful to Christianity were put to death by being burned at the stake. Probably all the men with Cortés had seen men and women executed in this awful manner. It could be argued that burning people at the stake was the Spanish version of human sacrifice. However the Spaniards never made a connection between their religious practices and Mexican human sacrifice. Therefore native human sacrifice remained in Spanish minds a pagan and sinful rite.

Several Totonac warriors, indignant because of the desecration of their gods, drew their bows and aimed arrows at the Spaniards. Cortés seized the fat cacique and threatened to kill him if one arrow was fired. An uneasy peace prevailed, and the Totonacs and the Spaniards remained allies.

Soon the Aztec dignitaries returned bearing gifts from Montezuma. One brought the soldier's helmet, and indeed it was filled with gold dust and gold pieces. The other gifts carried by Montezuma's representatives were fabulous. Bernal Díaz, one of Cortés's men, wrote:

> The first article presented was a wheel like the sun, as big as a cartwheel, with many sorts of pictures on it, the whole of fine gold, and a wonderful thing to behold. Then another wheel was presented of greater size made of silver . . . Then were brought twenty golden ducks, beautifully worked and very natural looking.

Item after item was paraded before Cortés. The gold and silver, the artwork, and the brilliance of the pieces were spellbinding. The men of Spain marveled over this Aztec treasure.

Cortés acted appreciative but not overwhelmed by the presents. He gave the ambassadors gifts of his own, glassware and a finely fashioned armchair, to present to Montezuma. Most important he still insisted on going to Tenochtitlán and speaking to the Aztec chief in person. Cortés would not compromise on that demand.

On June 28, 1519, the Spaniards held a ceremony to formally found the town they called Villa Rica de la Vera Cruz (Rich Village of the True Cross). Cortés then began stripping his ships of lumber in order to construct buildings in the new town. Some reports say he burned his fleet, but many historians discount that story. He did render his ships unseaworthy, and did this for a sound reason: The ships represented an escape path back to the safety and security of Cuba. He was determined to march into the heartland of the Aztecs, the mightiest military power in Mexico. Many Spanish soldiers would no doubt suffer faintness of heart during this mission and wish to turn back. With the ships destroyed their escape route was closed. The men had no choice but to follow their commander to death if necessary.

All of Cortés's moves were observed by Montezuma. The Aztecs had no draft animals such as horses and oxen which could be used to pull carts. For that reason they used the wheel only for jewelry or for making children's toys. Still they carved out roads and footpaths in every part of their empire and kept in communication with runners. The runners were specially trained since boyhood. Each runner raced over footpaths to post houses spaced about five miles apart. At the post house one runner gave a written message to another, who sped the message to the next link in the chain. In this manner messages were carried from the Veracruz area two hundred and fifty miles to the capital in just twenty-four hours.

Messages told Montezuma of Cortés's activities in the Totonac lands, where he gave the people a new god whose symbol was a cross and he preached against human sacrifice. Quetzalcoatl of old also condemned human sacrifice. Was there now any question remaining? This stranger was the god Quetzalcoatl, and he intended to claim all of Mexico as his realm. Emperor Montezuma would be forced to vacate his throne. Certainly no mortal man can fight a god and deny that god his will.

FIVE

The March Inland

On August 8, 1519, Cortés set off on his bold march to the Aztec capital. Accounts vary, but he began the trip with about four hundred Spanish soldiers and sixteen horses. Marching with the Spaniards were some one thousand Totonac warriors. Cortés left a contingent of one hundred men, mainly the old and the sick, at the Veracruz settlement. He wished to keep the Veracruz port open to receive more Spanish ships.

With this small force Cortés hoped to journey inland more than two hundred miles and defeat the greatest military power in the region. It was one of the most ambitious and daring military efforts in all of world history. Even Bernal Díaz, a humble soldier in the ranks, marveled at his own men and the mission they were about to undertake. He wrote, "What men have there been in the world who have shown such daring?"

Years later Cortés wrote the Spanish king a letter about the beginning of his expedition. The tone of the letter makes it clear he was trying to enhance his own reputation and win royal favors: "In my last letter, Most Excellent Prince, I told you of all the cities and towns I conquered for you. I also mentioned that the natives of this country had told me about a great lord called Montezuma . . . Trusting in the greatness of God and the power of your Royal name, I decided to go see him, and I vowed that I would have him prisoner or dead or subject to Your Majesty."

Fears, hopes, and prayers swirled through the minds of every Spaniard on the march. Most men dreamed of the treasure waiting for them. Bernal Díaz once wrote, "We came here to serve God and the king, and also to get rich." Spanish soldiers were paid in booty, a sum based on the amount of gold their army could loot. The king must be paid his fifth, and the officers would take their large shares. But it was believed the Aztec nation offered booty so abundant that even the common soldier would become a rich man. Beyond wealth, the Spaniards believed they were serving God by

Soldier With a Pen

Bernal Díaz del Castillo (1492-1581) was one of Cortés' most reliable soldiers. He also served on the two previous missions to Mexico, making him one of the most experienced of the conquistadors. When he was an old man living in present-day Guatemala he wrote his memoirs: *True History of The Discovery And Conquest Of Mexico*. Díaz's book is written in a matter-of-fact style and carries the voice of the common soldiers, who were usually dirty and hungry. Many other accounts of the conquistadors, including those of Cortés, are boastful and tend to self-glamorize the writer. Bernal Díaz' book is a valuable tool for historians and an interesting read for all students of Mexico's past.

bringing the word of Christ to the heathens. Each soldier felt, deep in his heart, that God was on his side.

After a two-week trek the army passed through a city called Zautla. The people of the city had heard of the Spaniards, but this was the first time they actually saw the outsiders with their monster horses and dogs and their cannon. They were told the dogs bit anyone who annoyed the Spaniards, the horses ran down anyone attempting to flee from them, and the cannons killed at a distance. The chief of Zautla said, "Well, [the Spaniards] must be gods then."

Stretching out before the Spaniards were jagged mountains as far as their eyes could see. The rugged landscape and the sheer distance of their goal, the Aztec capital, must have discouraged at least some of them. Just a few months ago most of the soldiers believed this land called Mexico was just another island in the Caribbean Sea. Now endless miles of mountains and forests stood between them and the great city they wished to visit.

This map traces Cortes's route through Mexico to Tenochtitlan.

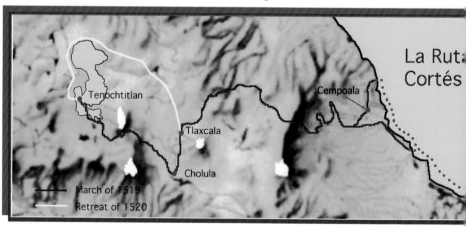

Cortés's first destination was the region called Tlaxcala. His Totonac allies said the Tlaxcalans were also enemies of the Aztecs. Cortés was a shrewd diplomat, quick to spot divisions among the Indian peoples and attempt to play one tribe against the other. While marching towards Tlaxcala he was in continual contact with Montezuma's emissaries. Montezuma, at this point, was clearly confused as to how to deal with Cortés and the approaching Spanish army. The Aztec emperor went through spells where he hoped to be Cortés's friend and other spells where he plotted against him as an enemy.

The first contact with the Tlaxcalans was violent, as fighting broke out between a small band of Tlaxcalans and an advance party of Spaniards. Perhaps the Spaniards would have suffered grave losses in this first encounter, but they were saved by the peculiar Mexican method of fighting. The Tlaxcalans and other Mexican warriors tried to stun their foes with clubs and then drag them away while they were still living. Sturdy hearts of soldiers made fine food for the gods, and Tlaxcalan priests wanted live men for their altars. By contrast, Spanish swordsmen and spearmen fought for the quick kill, jabbing at chests and throats.

The warriors were finally driven off, but two valuable horses were killed in the skirmish. The body of one horse was carried off by the Tlaxcalans. Cortés ordered the other dead horse to be buried immediately. He was aware of the godlike status he enjoyed among the Mexicans, and he did not want tribes to know that the horses were mortal.

The next morning the Spaniards faced an army of thousands of Tlaxcalans, standing in ranks, their faces smeared with war paint. "All the plain was swarming with warriors," wrote Bernal Díaz. Banging on drums, shrieking, and blowing conch shell trumpets the Tlaxcalans raced at the much smaller Spanish army. "How they began to charge on us! What a hail of stones sped from their slings."

Spanish cannons opened fire. The enemy attacked in such tight formations that one cannonball brought down scores of them. The battle lasted for hours. Blood soaked the ground. The Tlaxcalans finally retreated after several key commanders were killed. The end of combat was welcomed by the Spaniards, "whose arms were weary from killing Indians."

Despite the victory Spanish morale sank to its lowest ebb. Almost all the men nursed wounds. Cortés himself was sick with a fever. They were camped on a mountaintop, and every night cold winds lashed their flimsy tents and huts. Also the Tlaxcalans changed their tactics and launched several attacks after dark.

Talk spread, even among top Spanish officers, that the expedition should march back to Veracruz and find some way to return to Cuba. Mexico was not the Caribbean. It was madness to think that their small force could conquer this vast land and so many thousands of people. Cortés wrote, "I even heard some of the men say that if I had gone mad and was going where I could never escape, they didn't have to do the same, but should return instead to the seacoast."

With gloom overwhelming the army, Cortés faced a mutiny. Then a miracle saved the Spaniards and Captain Cortés. Tlaxcalan soldiers also suffered from dismally low morale. They believed the horses and magical weapons employed by the Spaniards made their foe invincible. Emissaries from Tlaxcala approached the Spanish camp asking for peace. They claimed that their leaders had met and decided their forces

The Tlaxcalans escort a Spanish soldier.

could not beat the Spanish army. Cortés was delighted. Peace with the Tlaxcalans had been his goal from the beginning.

The Spaniards were allowed into Tlaxcala, the capital city. To their astonishment they were treated like heroes. They were given turkeys to eat. Even the dogs were fed turkeys. Talks were held. Cortés learned that the Tlaxcalans hated the Aztecs because of the tributes they demanded in both goods and sacrificial victims.

For twenty days the Spaniards stayed in Tlaxcala. According to Gómara, "The lords of Tlaxcala performed a thousand kindnesses for the Spaniards and showed Cortés every courtesy." The Spaniards toured the city, and noted its well-run markets and orderly streets. Cortés wrote his king, "There is a market in which every day more than thirty thousand souls sell and buy . . . There are jewelry shops for gold. Silver, stones, and other valuables . . . There is also as

Malinche and Cortés meet the Tlaxcalans.

good earthenware and crockery as the best in Spain . . . And in all this good order and politeness prevail, for they are a people full of intelligence and understanding."

The long and welcome rest in Tlaxcala cured the Spaniards of their depression and defeatism. The march to Tenochtitlán resumed with renewed spirit. Most of the battle-weary Totonacs were sent home. The Spanish ranks now swelled with more than 6,000 fresh Tlaxcalan soldiers.

Before leaving Tlaxcala, Cortés obeyed Spanish law and read the *requiriemiento* (requirement) to the people.

He solemnly did this at every new city he encountered. The *requiriemiento* was a written declaration which said the land was now claimed by Spain and the people were subjects of the Spanish king. As Spanish citizens, the natives were required to abandon their old beliefs and accept Christianity as the only true religion. Conquistadors read this declaration in the Caribbean regions when they landed on new islands. On the islands the words were recited by a priest in Spanish or Latin, leaving the natives thoroughly bewildered.

At Tlaxcala the *requirimiento* was read perfectly in the Nahuatl language by Malinche. Still the Tlaxcalans did not understand the true meaning behind the words. How could a king who lived across a wide ocean govern them? And how could only one god keep the universe functioning in proper order? It was too much work to expect a single deity to bring the rains as well as the sunlight needed to grow crops. People should worship a rain god as well as a god of the sun if they wanted to prosper. The Tlaxcalans listened to the *requirieminto*, but secretly many concluded the Spaniards were madmen or fools.

Montezuma was informed of the Tlaxcala victory. Once more the Aztec emperor changed his method of dealing with the approaching Spaniards. He sent emissaries to Cortés bearing more gifts of gold, and this time invited the Europeans to Tenochtitlán. Montezuma suggested the Spaniards come through the city of Cholula, a fortified mountain town that was under Aztec control. The people of Cholula worshipped many gods, but most important in their hearts was Quetzalcóatl. It was believed that hundreds of years ago Quetzalcóatl lived in Cholula and served as that city's king. Montezuma had a dream that Cortés—although he was surely a god—would be stopped at Cholula.

Valley of
Mexico
circa 1900
(*Library of
Congress*)

Cortés and his party trekked through farm regions, green with corn. Farmers stopped their work to gape at the soldiers, their armor, and their horses. The horses always drew wondrous attention. Indian people heard the Spaniards talking to their horses and they assumed the animals could talk back. It was early October 1519. The army neared the Valley of Mexico, the country's fertile heartland.

Pleasant Valley with a Flaw

The Valley of Mexico enjoys one of the most pleasant climates found anywhere on earth. Though the region is in the tropical zone, temperatures are springlike most of the year. The valley is roughly 7,000 feet above sea level, so the weather is rarely hot and humid. The only flaw in this bright climate picture is a lack of rain. Rainfall in central Mexico is seasonal. The rainy season begins in early June and lasts through October. In ancient times and in the modern era a poor rainy season spells disaster for farmers. It is no wonder that Tlaloc, the rain god, was one of the most important deities for all the peoples in the region.

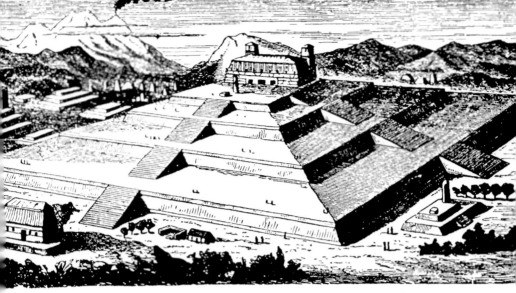

Drawing of the City of Cholula and one of its mighty pyramids

At the gates of Cholula, the Spanish-led army was greeted by musicians playing flutes and beating drums. Children ceremoniously scattered flowers over the path leading to the city gates. Leaders welcomed Cortés in apparent friendship. But his new Tlaxcalan allies told him to be wary of these people, as the Cholulans were terrified of the Aztecs and would obey their every command. Cortés's suspicion was aroused when the leaders invited the Spaniards into the city, but requested their Indian allies remain in the outskirts. Cortés agreed to the request while cautioning his men to remain alert.

Cholula was a thousand-year-old city. It was here, according to legends, where Quezalcoatl once ruled and told the people not to sacrifice humans. The city remained a religious center and was made up of mighty pyramids and temples. Cortés counted 430 pyramids in Cholula. The city also had a broad marketplace where food and excellent pottery were sold. He told the king that Cholula was, "more beautiful than anything in Spain."

On the third day of their stay the Cholulans quit bringing food to the Spaniards. City chiefs failed to attend conferences with Cortés and his officers. Cortés made a speech and

73

Malinche dutifully read the requiremiento. No one seemed to listen. Bernal Díaz claimed, "[They] remained some distance off, laughing at us as though mocking us."

It was in Cholula where Malinche saved the Cortés expedition. One night an elderly woman, the wife of a Cholulan leader, approached her. The woman said she admired Malinche and wished to warn her to get out of the city. The Cholulans planned a sneak attack and would kill everyone in the Spanish party. The attack had been ordered by Montezuma himself. The woman further warned that at this moment there were 20,000 Aztec soldiers poised outside the city, ready to rush in and participate in the assault. Malinche reported all this information to Cortés.

Once more Cortés played the consummate actor. He called for an assembly of city noblemen and pretended he knew nothing of the plot. The assembly took place in the courtyard of the great temple of Quetzalcóatl. More than one hundred high chiefs came to the assembly, unarmed. Cortés then locked the courtyard gates. Angrily he told the leaders he knew of the plot and accused them all of treachery. The chiefs were shocked. This man could read minds! Some of the noblemen admitted their guilt, but claimed it was all Montezuma's fault. Montezuma would have them all killed if they failed to launch an attack on the Spaniards.

Cortés ordered a soldier with an arquebus to fire into the crowd of chiefs. That first gunshot was a signal for a massacre to begin: "*Santiago y a ellos!* / *"Santiago! Santiago!"*

Swordsmen raced into the packed group of noblemen who were trapped inside the temple compound. Unable to defend themselves the Cholulan leaders were cut down. Spaniards also attacked the people who had gathered outside the temple

The Spanish Army fought a fierce battle in Cholula.

walls. Writing to his king months later Cortés coldly said, "we did such an execution that in two hours more than three thousands people were killed."

And the slaughter continued. In a planned attack the Tlaxcalan allies fought their way into the city, murdering and looting. Bernal Díaz wrote, "The Tlaxcalans went about the city, plundering and making prisoners and we could not stop them, and the next day more companies from the Tlaxacalan town arrived, and did great damage, for they were very hostile to the people of Cholula."

When the massacre finally ended the Tlaxcalans marched away all prisoners in order to sacrifice them at their altars. Cortés, of course, condemned human sacrifice as a vile sin against God. But he needed the Tlaxcalans as allies. So, he simply looked the other way as they practiced their old ways.

About 6,000 people from Cholula were killed in a morning of horror. The event was a major reason why future Mexican historians branded Cortés as a mass murderer. Why the Spanish chief had to extract so much blood in order to punish the Cholula conspirators remains a subject of debate. Perhaps he wanted to impress Montezuma that he was no man—or god—who would tolerate being tricked. Perhaps he lost control of his own soldiers and his allies, who engaged in a reckless frenzy of killing. Or perhaps the massacre at Cholula was a symptom of the era, when cruelty and bloodletting were the norm.

The Spanish Army battled numerous Indian tribes on its way through Mexico.

Word about the military defeat and massacre in Cholula soon reached Tenochtitlán. Now everyone in the Aztec capital, not just Montezuma, waited in dread for the coming of these angry gods who looked like men. An Aztec said, "The common people were terrified . . . they could do nothing but tremble with fright. It was as if the earth trembled beneath them, or as if the world was spinning before their eyes . . ."

Cortés manipulated the situation as if it were a political chess game. At first he told Montezuma's ambassadors that he was furious at the Aztec chief for the alleged plot against him and his men. The ambassadors said the planned sneak attack had not been ordered by Montezuma, but instead was the idea of a local Aztec general. Cagily, Cortés accepted this explanation. He was more determined than ever to go to Tenochtitlán, and he hoped that his initial approach at least would be made in an atmosphere of peace.

SIX

Cortés and Montezuma

The Aztec capital lies only fifty miles from Cholula, but in Mexico mighty mountains block the paths of all creatures except the birds. Tlaxcalan traders acted as guides for the Cortés party and led the army through mountain passes.

Near Cholula Cortés saw what he described as, "two very high and marvelous mountains [whose] tops were completely covered with snow. From the highest one a great volume of smoke thick as a house comes forth." Few if any members of the expedition had ever seen an active volcano before. Cortés sent two men who he thought were his best climbers to the top of the highest mountain to investigate, but because of the snow and ice and the clouds of smoke the men could not reach the peak.

The Twin Volcanoes

The mountains that so impressed Cortés were two giant volcanoes with the tongue-twisting names Popocatépetl (The Hill that Smokes) and Iztaccíhuatl (The White Woman). Years ago the snowcapped mountains could be seen clearly through the thin clear air of Mexico City. A story was told that the mountains were husband and wife. They were madly in love with each other, but argued frequently. When they quarreled thunder and lightening rocked the city. Mexico City is now one of the most polluted urban centers in the world. The city sits in a bowl, ringed by tall mountains which trap pollutants in the air. Because of fumes coming from factories and motor vehicles the two magnificent volcanoes are almost never seen by present-day Mexico City residents.

The army moved with deliberate caution and rested frequently. Couriers sent by Montezuma brought them supplies of turkeys, eggs, and tortillas. The men were fascinated by their surroundings. Rich forests gave way to green farmland and small well-built villages. Lakes dotted the region. The Spaniards passed many chinampas, the unique farms built on artificial islands.

The men of Spain encountered the town of Iztapalapa, which was built with half the houses on dry land and the other half on stilts in lake waters. Cortés said the houses of Iztapalapa were, "as good as the best in Spain from the point of view of masonry. They are as large and as well constructed, not only in the stone work but also in the wood work."

Lakes in an Arid Land

The presence of lakes would suggest the Valley of Mexico enjoyed ample rainfall, however that was not the case. The valley has no natural outlets so the rain that does fall gathers in lakes. Because of the ground the lakes have a salt content making their waters unsuitable for drinking, but useable for crop irrigation. Centuries ago lakes in the Valley of Mexico were drained as the capital city expanded. Mexico, once an island city, now suffers a chronic water shortage.

Montezuma's fears and feelings of impending doom increased as the Spanish army neared his capital. He refused food, shut himself up in his palace, and prayed. The Emperor ordered special sacrifices, and scores of hapless victims were led to the altars and to their deaths. Montezuma reasoned that if rival gods were sated with many human hearts they would drive these foreigners away from the city.

To Montezuma's dismay, the gods refused to intervene and the Spanish army kept marching towards his capital. He sent gifts to the Spaniards hoping they would simply take them and go back where they came from. One emissary delivered a particularly large load of gold and noted the Spaniards' reaction: "Like monkeys, they seized upon the gold . . . For in truth they thirsted mightily, they stuffed themselves with it, and starved and lusted for it like pigs. They . . . showed it to one another all the while babbling. What they said was gibberish."

Showering the Spaniards with gifts of gold had the reverse effect from Montezuma's wishes. By presenting gold, the emperor advertised his wealth. Every gift excited the Spaniards and made them more determined to grasp the ultimate prize, the grand treasure they were certain they would find in Tenochtitlán.

Emperor Montezuma issued orders for the people in neighboring towns to ignore the approaching Spaniards. Normally the townsmen were obedient, but in this case curiosity overwhelmed them and they lined the pathways to see the strangers. These were gods, or so it appeared, marching with their strange animals and heavy cannon. The people could not help but look upon them with awe and greet the foreigners with polite gestures. It was as though men from another planet were visiting Earth for the first time.

On November 8, 1519, almost three months after leaving Veracruz, Cortés approached the main causeway which led to Tenochtitlán. The causeways were roads made of huge stones and cement which were built in the waters of Lake Texcoco to allow foot traffic to reach the city. Three major causeways connected the capital city with the lakeshores.

The Spanish army enters Tenochtitlan over a causeway.

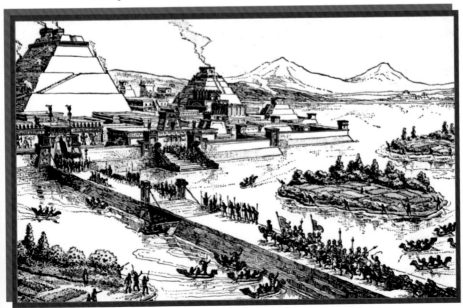

Cortés said the causeways were wide enough for eight men to easily march side by side.

At various intervals the straight and level causeways were broken by wooden bridges which could be removed to allow canoe and barge traffic to pass. All Spanish soldiers noted that the bridges could also be taken away in order to trap an invading army in the city. However the excitement they felt and the wonder of their surroundings drowned the men's fears. Bernal Díaz wrote, "I do not know how to describe it, seeing things as we did that had never been seen before, not even dreamed about."

As they proceeded the waters on both sides of the causeway became black with canoes. The canoes, built from hollowed-out logs, were filled with people who had come to watch the spectacle. Some canoes held up to sixty men and women, who saw the grandest parade of their lives.

Four horsemen marched in front, leading the parade over the causeway. They were followed by a foot soldier carrying the Spanish flag. He waved the flagpole in circles, making the banner flutter in the breeze. More foot soldiers followed, armed with swords, spears, crossbows, or arquebuses. The men wore armor which sparkled like mirrors in the morning sunlight. Cortés and several other officers on horseback brought up the rear of the infantrymen. Behind them marched 7,000 Indian allies, mostly Tlaxcalans. The Tlaxcalans whistled and shouted war whoops as they entered the capital city of their arch enemy, seemingly in triumph.

A huge throng awaited the parade at the point where the causeway ended and the houses of the island city began. Gómara wrote, "so many people were crowded at the doors and windows and on the roofs [of the houses] that I know not who was the more amazed, our men at seeing such a multitude of men and women in the city, or they at the guns, horses, beards, and dress of our men, such as they had never seen before."

Respectfully the crowd parted as a group of Aztec dignitaries came forward. These principal citizens who Cortés described as "richly dressed" dropped to their knees, put a hand on the ground, and then kissed it. This Aztec gesture of respect was repeated by one nobleman after another.

Finally came Montezuma. There was no mistaking him. He was the only one wearing shoes, and his were sandals with gold soles and precious jewels embedded in the upper straps. He walked under a canopy held by a team of lords. The canopy itself was a work of art, made of bright green feathers with braces of gold and silver.

Confidently, Cortés stepped up to the emperor with the intent of giving him the traditional Spanish abrazo (hug), but the accompanying Aztec lords stopped him. No one was

Cortés meeting Montezuma *(Courtesy of the Rare Book and Special Collections Division, Library of Congress)*

allowed such close contact with the emperor. Montezuma and Cortés did shake hands, and this alone shocked the onlookers. No Aztec would even dare look the emperor directly in the face much less touch his hand.

Montezuma had tried bribery, trickery, and warfare to avoid this meeting with the white god. Now that the meeting was forced upon him, he treated Cortés as what he believed he was—a returning god. According to an Aztec account Montezuma said through Malinche, who was always at Cortés's side, "No, it is not a dream. I am not walking in my sleep. I am not seeing you in my dreams. I have seen you at last! I have met you face to face! I was in agony for five days, for ten days, with my eyes fixed on the Region of the Mystery. And now you have come out of the clouds and mists to sit on your throne again."

Montezuma then suggested the Spaniards should rest and eat. Cortés and his men were led to their quarters, a huge palace that once belonged to Montezuma's father. They were fed lavishly. Their horses were given beds of flowers.

After dinner, Montezuma gave a speech. He told the story of Quetzalcóatl, and how the Aztec people had always known the god would someday come back. Montezuma now claimed the Spanish king, if not Cortés himself, was indeed Quetzalcóatl of old. Graciously Emperor Montezuma said he would surrender his throne: "From what you tell of your great lord, or king, who has sent you here, we believe, and hold for certain, that he is our rightful sovereign . . . Hence you may be sure that we shall always obey you."

That night Cortés celebrated his triumphant entrance to the capital by firing a cannon in the middle of the city's main square. The cannon salute stunned the residents. According to

The market at Tenochtitlan

an Aztec wrier, "Then the Spaniards fired one of their cannons, and this caused great confusion in the city. The people scattered in every direction . . . they ran off as if they were being pursued . . . their fears would not let them sleep."

Over the next few days the men were free to explore the city. Holding about 250,000 people, it was far larger than any city in Europe. Never before had the Spaniards seen such marvels: tall pyramids, broad streets, canals, palaces; and fine houses of the rich. To the Europeans it was more a dreamscape than a real city. Everything was kept remarkably clean by an army of street sweepers and men who hauled away all waste.

The marketplace held a special fascination. Some of the Spaniards had been to Rome, which was famed for its lively market area. The market here was far larger and held a far greater variety of goods.

Everyday some 60,000 people came to the market plaza, which lay almost in the shadow of the city's largest pyramid. Merchandise was kept in perfect order with each item in its proper section. Honey was sold in one row of booths, rubber in another, and pottery in still another. Barbers cut hair in a particular corner while dentists pulled aching teeth in a nearby section. Food vendors sold ducks, turkeys, fish, tortillas, and corn cakes spiced with chili peppers (called tamales). Buyers browsed through clothes made from cotton and dyed in colorful patterns. Slaves were sold in a designated place. The slaves had their hands tied behind their backs and attached to long poles to make escape difficult.

Goods were bartered because the Aztecs had no coinage. Sometimes cacao beans were used as a form of currency. The market had special courts where judges ruled on disputes between traders. Thieves or anyone determined to have sold stolen goods were executed, often by having their heads crushed by a muscular man wielding a stone club. Entertainment thrived in the marketplace. Shoppers watched music and dancing shows which were given throughout the plaza.

Naturally the goods made from gold drew the Spaniards' attention. Many of Cortés's soldiers were disappointed because they saw only jewelry. In their dreams they had expected to find houses made from gold bricks in the Aztec capital. However they were astonished by the outstanding work they saw in the jewelry. A Spanish priest said these craftsmen were superior to, "goldsmiths in Spain, inasmuch as they can cast a bird with a movable head, tongue, and feet and . . . a toy with which seems to dance."

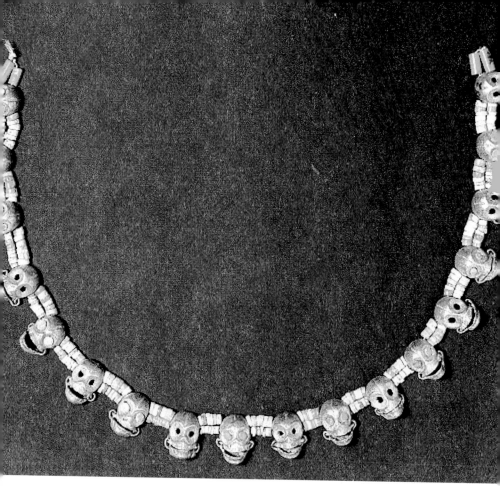

An Aztec necklace

Surviving Art

Very few pieces of the wonderful Aztec gold statues and ornaments have survived and are now in museums. The Spaniards quickly melted all the gold objects of art that were given to them or that they looted. They had to melt the pieces in order to distribute the booty among themselves and to make sure the king was sent his one-fifth share. Also the Aztec gold statues often represented their gods who Spaniards thought to be devils. The melting down process destroyed forever the exquisite works fashioned by Aztec artists centuries ago.

The Aztecs, they would learn, did not value gold with the same passion as did Europeans. To the Aztecs rare and colorful feathers were more highly prized than gold. The market held hats and blouses made from exotic feathers, all intricately woven together. Bernal Díaz was awed by the, "the Indian women who . . . made such an immense quantity of fine fabrics with wonderful feather work design." Most other Spaniards found the feathered items to be interesting, but not exciting—certainly not compared to gold.

Some of the men were privileged to visit Emperor Montezuma's private zoo. The aviary alone contained hundreds of birds singing and flapping about in cages. These birds were captured in every part of the vast Aztec Empire, including the rain forests to the south. Bernal Díaz said there were, "birds which have feathers of five colors—green, red, white, yellow, and blue . . . there were parrots of many different colors . . . not to mention the beautifully marked ducks." Also caged at the zoo were wolves, bears, jaguars, and foxes. One section was devoted to snakes and their hissing, according to Díaz, "was horrible to listen to and seemed like a hell." Finally a portion of the zoo was given over to dwarfs and hunchbacks. Emperor Montezuma found people with deformities to be amusing and frequently had them dance before him.

Despite the beauties of the city, the Aztec religion troubled the Spaniards. Signs of it were everywhere. In a courtyard near the great pyramid, there stood a long rack which held endless rows of human skulls. They were the skulls of sacrificial victims, and now they stared grimly into eternity. Since the skulls were placed in uniform rows they could be quickly counted. One soldier counted the number of skulls in one row and multiplied by the other rows he saw. The soldier claimed the rack held 136,000 skulls.

One morning a group of Spaniards, including Bernal Díaz, were given a tour of the city's tallest pyramid and the temple complex on its truncated top. The tour was organized and guided by Emperor Montezuma himself. First the group climbed up the side of the pyramid, which was an exhausting ascent. The steps were built deliberately steep for a reason. Humans were sacrificed on the top of the pyramid and their lifeless bodies thrown down the sides. The steep steps allowed the bodies to tumble unheeded all the way to the ground below.

Several high-ranking Aztecs carried Montezuma in a litter up the pyramid while the panting Spaniards climbed. Upon reaching the flat surface on top the group beheld a magnificent view of the capital. Below spread the checkerboard pattern of streets, the three broad causeways, and the sparkling

A skull rack, or tzomplantli, made from the skulls of sacrificial victims

lakes surrounding the island city. It was a breathtaking sight and confirmed the belief of many Spaniards that the Aztec capital was the grandest city on earth.

Montezuma invited the Spaniards into one of the two temples on top of the pyramid. He chose the one devoted to Huitzilopochtli, the hummingbird, the terrible god of war. What Cortés and his men saw inside horrified and sickened them. Bernal Díaz described the hummingbird's statue: "it had a very broad face and monstrous and terrible eyes . . . and the body was girdled by great snakes . . . All the walls of the oratory were so splashed and encrusted with blood that they were black, the floor was the same and the whole place stank vilely."

Behind the statue was a ferocious figure of a creature, half man half lizard. In front of the idol were bowls which held the still warm hearts of human beings who had been sacrificed just that morning. Even the priests accompanying Montezuma were frightful sights. Religious law forbade them from bathing or cutting their hair. After years of cutting open chests to extract living hearts, their long hair was matted and tangled with dried blood.

Courtesy had been the rule between Cortés and Montezuma, but during this tour an argument broke out between the two men. Years later Bernal Díaz recalled their discourse. Through the interpreters, Cortés said, "Senior Montezuma, I do not understand how such a great Prince and wise man as you are has not come to the conclusion in your mind that these idols of yours are not gods, but evil things that are called devils . . ." At those remarks Montezuma became angry and said, "If I had known that you would have said such defamatory things I would not have shown you my gods, we consider them to be very good, for they give us health and rains and good seed times and as many victories as we desire and we are obliged to worship them and make sacrifices, and I pray you not to not to say another word to their dishonor." Cortés apologized and the Spaniards descended down the pyramid side. They were shaken by their experience and decided to build a chapel to the Virgin Mary in their quarters. There they could worship and cleanse themselves of any sin that may have stained their souls during the visit to the pagan temple. The search for the chapel site led to still another stroke of luck for the Cortés expedition.

An experienced carpenter named Alonso Yanez was given the job of building the shrine to the Virgin Mary. While looking about the castle that served as their home, Yanez noticed marks on the floor that indicated a door had recently

A European painting of the temple of Huitzilopochtli and its priests, with a statue of the god near the back

Aztec priests sacrifice a victim to the god Huitzilopochtli by removing the heart. *(Library of Congress)*

been sealed up with bricks. Men tore the bricks down and made the discovery of their lives. Inside was a hidden room overflowing with objects of gold, jade, precious gems, and fine feather work. The gold included cups and large plates. Bernal Díaz said, "I took it for certain that there could not be another such store of wealth in the whole world." These precious goods once belonged to Montezuma's father, Axayacatl, and Montezuma himself had them sealed in the secret chamber. Finally the men had found a cache of riches to match their fantasies.

Cortés ordered the chamber to be resealed and the gold left untouched. There was time enough later to distribute this fortune among the men. The always bold Hernando Cortés pondered a new plan and he was about to make his boldest move of all.

SEVEN

The Captive Nation

On November 8, the sixth day of their stay in the capital, Cortés and a group of officers paid a visit to Montezuma. The meeting began with friendly conversation. Then, suddenly, Cortés exploded in a fit of rage. He said he had received word that his garrison at Veracruz was attacked by Aztec soldiers and several Spaniards were killed in battle. Actually Cortés had known about the battle for at least two days. Montezuma too had heard of the attack and he claimed he had not ordered any such military action.

The Veracruz incident was a pretext for Cortés' next move. He told Montezuma he was now a prisoner of the Spaniards and if he resisted he would be killed on the spot. Cortés was flanked by officers, all of whom carried swords. Montezuma was surrounded mostly by unarmed lords and noblemen. The Aztec emperor then did something unbefitting such a powerful man: he cried. Through his tears he agreed to go with the Spaniards, anything to avoid an armed clash. Montezuma was led away in chains, to the shock and bewilderment of his people.

History has shown that the most audacious plan imaginable sometimes can succeed simply because of its shock value. Certainly a miracle of sorts took place in Tenochtitlán on November 8, 1519. The Spaniards were outnumbered at least 250 to 1 by Aztec soldiers. They were hundreds of miles away from their nearest base at Veracruz, and thousands of miles from Spain. Yet they succeeded in capturing Montezuma in his own palace.

In this seemingly mad venture Cortés was aided by a weakness in Aztec society: the people's obedience to authority. No doubt Cortés perceived this weakness and counted on it to carry out his operation. The Aztecs were highly disciplined men and women. They would obey Montezuma's orders even if it meant their death. Montezuma, for his part, was in awe of the Spaniards. Cortés was aware of this also. He hoped the emperor would be confused by the brazen act of taking him prisoner.

The scheme worked with uncanny perfection. The bewildered Montezuma issued no orders. The Aztecs did nothing. Cortés took an outrageous gamble that November morning in the year 1519. And, temporarily at least, he won an empire.

A strange six months passed. Montezuma was a prisoner of the Spaniards, yet he was allowed the image of rule. He received ambassadors from vassal states, appointed judges, and presided over religious festivals. These were the same tasks he performed since he was made emperor many years ago. Still he was held a virtual captive. He resided in the castle of Axayacatl, which was the Spanish quarters, instead of his own castle. Spanish guards watched over him night and day.

Cortés insisted his men treat Montezuma with the utmost respect and dignity. When one soldier was rude to the emperor Cortés ordered the man to be flogged. A teenage page boy with the Spanish army became a Montezuma favorite. The boy learned a few words in the Nahuatl language, which he pronounced badly, causing Montezuma to laugh. The emperor was allowed all his accustomed pleasures. Regularly he was entertained by musicians and dancers and by his favorite jugglers and court jesters. He was permitted a trip to his zoo any time he wished to go.

Montezuma was forty-one years old, two years older than Cortés. Bernal Díaz described him as being, "of good height and well proportioned, slender . . . His face was somewhat long, but cheerful, and he had good eyes." Cortés always wrote about him in honorable terms, often calling him a "Great Lord." Certainly the Spaniards were aware of the profound respect the Aztec people paid to their emperor. In a letter to King Charles, Cortés said, "No prince in the world was ever feared as he was by his subjects . . . Within the city, he had residences so marvelous that it is impossible to speak of their excellence and grandeur."

Amazingly, Cortés and Montezuma—though one was a jailer and the other a prisoner—became friends. They went on hunting trips at an island which served as the emperor's private game reserve. They gambled together, playing an Aztec game of dice called *patolli*. In the dice game they bet pieces of gold and Montezuma did not seem to mind when Cortés cheated him. The two talked for many hours. Cortés told his captive of his ambitions to win still more worlds for the glory of Spain. Captain Cortés hinted he would like to command the fine Aztec army, equip it with European weapons, and conquer China, which he believed lay nearby.

Religion was their favorite subject of conversation. Cortés told the Aztec leader about Christ and the Virgin Mary. Montezuma said he would be happy to add this new god and new goddess to his pantheon, but they must take their places with the two thousand or so other Aztec deities. This, of course, was unacceptable to Cortés. When the two talked about their religious beliefs tears filled their eyes, as both became overcome with emotion. Still one could not convince the other that their God or gods were superior.

Despite his being held prisoner, Montezuma and his bloodstained priests were allowed to continue their old religious practices. Human sacrifices remained regular events in Tenochtitlán. Cortés wanted to preserve the peace. As he did with his Tlaxcalan allies, he simply looked the other way while the ritualistic killings took place.

Montezuma was shocked by the Spanish lust for gold. Cortés told him the Spanish king needed still more precious metal for his treasury. The emperor took the Spaniards to his private treasury in the zoo building. There in a hidden room he showed them a fortune in golden jewelry, goblets, and marvelously crafted statues. An Aztec observer told how the Spaniards reacted upon seeing these glittering items, "The Spaniards grinned like little beasts and patted each other with delight . . . they were slaves to their own greed. All of Montezuma's possessions were brought out: fine bracelets, necklaces with large stones, ankle rings with golden bells . . . everything that belonged to the king and was reserved to him only. They seized these treasures as if they were their own, as if this plunder were merely a stroke of good luck."

As the months passed Montezuma remained meek and compliant in the hands of his captors while the Aztec people grew resentful. No longer did Aztec commoners consider the outsiders to be gods. They required sleep and food like everyone else. When cut they bled, just like mortals.

However the Aztecs had no orders from above to rise up and drive the Europeans from the capital. Life continued in an almost normal fashion. The city functioned in its time-honored rhythms. Every morning the market filled with vendors. Sweepers kept the streets immaculate. Holidays were celebrated in the grand tradition of the Mexican fiesta. Yet anger burned in the people's hearts due to the dominating presence of the foreigners.

The first serious rebellion against Cortés's rule came not from the Aztecs, but from his own countrymen. In May of 1520, Cortés learned that a fleet of Spanish ships had landed in Veracruz and discharged some 1,400 soldiers. The army was commanded by Pánfilo de Narváez, a veteran officer who had helped conquer Cuba. The men were sent to Veracruz by Diego Velázquez, the governor of Cuba and Cortés's old friend. Velázquez was still furious with Cortés for departing from Cuba more than a year ago without his specific orders. He told Narváez to arrest the upstart Cortés and take him back to Cuba in chains.

News of a rival army in Veracruz could not have come at a worse time for Cortés. The Aztecs in Tenochtitlán were near revolt. Two noblemen, including Montezuma's nephew and his brother, were secretly organizing an attack against the Spaniards. Montezuma learned of the plot and, in another attempt to curry the favor of his jailer, informed Cortés of his relatives' plans. Cortés captured both the conspirators and held them in a dungeon.

Captain Cortés decided it was the Aztec religion and their demon gods who were stirring up rebellions against him. With a few dozen men he climbed to the top of the city's tallest pyramid, pushed aside the priests gathered at the temple, and had soldiers strike the statue of Huitzilopochtli with iron bars. He hoped to dash the statue into pieces and discard the remains. Even the passive Montezuma objected to this treatment of the idol. A compromise was reached. Priests were allowed to carry the statue away to safety and Cortés erected a cross in its place. This time violence was avoided, but a bitter memory lingered with the Aztec. The Spaniards had defiled the people's highest god. The Aztecs silently swore revenge.

Cortés next had to deal with the Spanish army in Veracruz. He took about half his men and marched toward the port settlement, leaving Pedro de Alvarado in charge of the garrison at Tenochtitlán. This proved to be a mistake. Alvarado fought with tigerlike fury in combat, but he was also hot-tempered and given to act before thinking.

In mid-May 1520, the Aztecs celebrated a traditional festival for the god Toxcatl. The ceremony marked the end of the dry season and the beginning of the hoped-for rainy season. Customs called for the noblemen to dance at the temple complex. Normally the Aztecs were a quiet, reserved people. But during the excitement of a festival their emotions burst forth in an explosion of joy and wild enthusiasm.

About four hundred men participated in the ceremonies while thousands of others watched. The nobles joined hands, and like a giant serpent danced around a small group of men who pounded on drums. Sweat glistened on skin as they gyrated to the drumbeats. They moved and swayed with such intensity it seemed as if they had become possessed by otherworldly spirits.

Watching this scene were Pedro de Alvarado and about sixty of his men. Alvarado was edgy. Malinche, a master spy, told him she had heard from townswomen that the Aztecs planned an uprising. Days earlier he saw many knives and pots in the plaza. The cooking instruments were there to prepare a feast following the festival. But Alvarado's Tlaxcalan friends claimed the Aztecs intended to kill the Spaniards, cook them in the pots, and eat them with garlic.

A wave of terror overcame the Spanish soldiers. They urged their commander to strike first and deliver a terrible blow to the

Spanish soldiers kill Aztec revelers during the festival for Toxcatl.

Aztecs before they could organize and fight. In the temple complex, the Aztec dancing grew wilder. Drumbeats pounded louder, ever louder. Alvarado ordered the gates of the temple courtyard to be closed. He then shouted the command: *"Santiago y a ellos!"*

Wielding swords the Spaniards swept into the dancers, all of whom were unarmed. *"Santiago! Santiago!"* Years later a Spanish priest named Bernardino de Sahagún interviewed a survivor of this attack who gave him a graphic account: "They surrounded those who danced . . . They struck off the arms of the one who beat the drums . . . and afterwards . . . his neck and head flew off . . . They pierced them all with their iron lances and they struck each one with the iron swords . . . The blood of the chieftains ran like water."

Now the Aztecs struck back. Thousands of them armed with clubs, sticks, and spears charged at the Spaniards. Alvarado ordered a retreat and raced his men back to their quarters

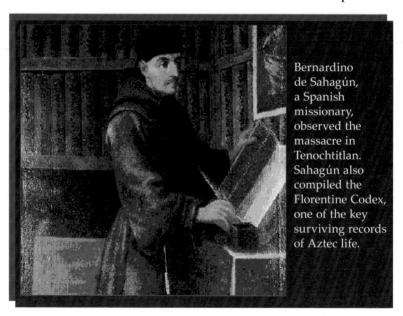

Bernardino de Sahagún, a Spanish missionary, observed the massacre in Tenochtitlan. Sahagún also compiled the Florentine Codex, one of the key surviving records of Aztec life.

Cortés captures and defeats Narváez.

in Axayacatl. They barred the doors while throngs outside chanted and screamed for their deaths. Finally a new noise rose from the streets: a chorus of men, women, and children stood mourning the many hundreds of dead. The sound of the mourners was so piteous that one Aztec reported, "[It] should have made the stones weep." In late May the rains came. The dry season ended. The rainy season began. As was hoped, the festival awakened the power of the gods.

Meanwhile Cortés, in Veracruz, enjoyed stunning success. He counted on Spanish greed and lust for gold to carry out a plot against Panfilo de Narváez. Cortés sent an advance party of two men to steal into the Narváez camp and tell the soldiers of the gold and other riches that awaited them in Tenochtitlán. The men were assured they could have a share in this wondrous booty if they simply rebelled against Narváez and joined Cortés's army.

It took little convincing for the men to act. They overthrew Narváez and after a brief fight proclaimed Cortés as their new leader. Once more the cunning Hernando Cortés had won the day. Narváez was left in chains at Veracruz. Cortés marched toward Tenochtitlán. His ranks now included hundreds of fresh, well-armed Spanish soldiers who once served his rival officer.

Days away from Tenochtitlán Cortés received word that some sort of uprising had rocked the Aztec capital. He cursed Pedro de Alvarado. The impetuous officer had ruined everything.

Cortés reached the capital in late June 1520. Torrential rains slowed the progress of his army. He found the streets and the outskirts of the city to be eerily silent and devoid of people. Marching up to the gate of Axayacatl Castle, the deathly stillness prevailed—everywhere.

Inside the castle Cortés discovered the remains of his once proud army. Now the soldiers were scared, starving, and virtual prisoners in their quarters. Worse yet, Cortés had fallen into the same trap. Outside, the streets suddenly filled with thousands of screaming Aztecs. Cortés too had become a prisoner in Axayacatl Castle.

For the next week the Spaniards fought a savage, desperate street battle in an attempt to regain control of the city. During the day the soldiers would secure a neighborhood near Axayacatl Castle, only to lose it at night to bands of Aztecs. Cannons were useless against them. A cannon shell might kill ten warriors, but in minutes one hundred men replaced those who fell. Even the veteran Bernal Díaz was overwhelmed by the enemy's fearlessness, "I declare that I do not know how to describe it, for neither cannon nor muskets nor crossbows availed, nor hand-to-hand fighting, nor killing thirty or forty of them every time we charged, for they still fought on in close ranks and with more energy than in the beginning."

In desperation Cortés asked Montezuma to speak to his people and persuade them to call off the war. Montezuma, the captive emperor, did as he was asked. He stood on a flat roof of the Spanish compound and called down to the Aztecs, imploring them to make peace with the Spaniards.

Remarkably the emperor was shouted down by the crowd below. Just months earlier, Montezuma was worshipped as a god. No Aztec would dare look him in the eyes much less shout curses at him. Now they cursed him, and above their angry yells came the name Cuauhtémoc. He was the emperor's nephew and had emerged as the nation's new leader. With Cuauhtémoc in charge the Aztecs once more had a military commander in place. When properly led, Aztec soldiers were a fearsome force.

What happened next is a matter of historical uncertainty. Spanish accounts say that while Montezuma stood on the roof pleading for peace he was hit with a shower of rocks thrown from the mob below. One rock struck him on the forehead and knocked him unconscious. Three days later he died. In a letter to King Charles, Cortés insisted this story of Montezuma's death was true: "one of his [Montezuma's] own subjects struck him on the head with such force that within three days he died." The Aztec account of Montezuma's death differs sharply from Spanish claims. According to

The Spanish claimed that a rock was thrown at Montezuma and killed him.

Aztec sources Montezuma and several other captives were hacked to death by Spanish swordsmen while they were in chains and helpless to defend themselves. The true circumstances regarding the death of the Aztec leader will never be known.

With food and water almost exhausted Cortés decided on a desperate plan. He ordered his men and his Tlaxcalan allies to break out of the castle at night, cross one of the causeways, and head for dry land on the opposite shore of Lake Texcoco. Cortés hoped he could use the cover of darkness to escape.

Silently the Spaniards prepared for the night operation. They faced a perplexing dilemma: what to do with the looted gold? Cortés brought the gold and silver from the treasury and placed it on the floor. The artwork had been melted down and the precious metal stored as ingots. Captain Cortés ordered the king's share to be placed on horses and told the men they could take what they could carry. The vast bulk of the treasure had to be left behind.

Cortés cautioned the soldiers that they must travel light during their escape. However all had crossed an ocean hoping to gain a fortune. How could they leave these glittering ingots behind? Most of the new men, who once served under Narváez, overburdened themselves with treasure. Some had packs so heavy with ingots they could hardly walk. Cortés's veterans shunned the gold in order to make their escape light-footed.

At first it seemed Cortés's daring escape plan might work. It was a dark and rainy night as the force left their castle and headed towards the causeway that led to the town of Tacuba. The Tacuba causeway was the nearest and the shortest route out of the capital. Men had tied cloth around their horses' hoofs in order to muffle the beats. The long column approached the first gap in the causeway and discovered the bridge had been removed. Cortés had anticipated the Aztecs would remove the bridges. While still in the castle he built a portable bridge and now ordered it put into place. The advance party crossed. The operation seemed to be going well.

Then an explosion of noise and fury rocked the night as sentries spotted the column. The huge snakeskin drum on top of the tall pyramid pounded out an alarm. Aztec war cries pierced the darkness. On both sides of the Tacuba causeway came canoes crowded with warriors who rained arrows on the Spaniards. Aztec foot soldiers raced over the causeway and attacked the rear of the column. The Aztec rage was such that the men disregarded their instinct to take captives and lashed out at the Spaniards with swords and clubs in a killing frenzy.

Many Spanish soldiers drowned when they were driven into canal waters by the Aztecs.

Cortés tried to lead his soldiers out of this trap and to the lake shore. Men and horses screamed in agony as they were hit with arrows. Warriors in canoes reached out, grabbed the Spaniards' legs, and dragged them onto their boats or into the waters. In the confusion and darkness many Spaniards slipped off the causeway. Greed killed. Those who loaded themselves down with gold ingots sank like stones. Gómara said, "So those who died, died rich, and their gold killed them."

The retreat over the causeway became a rout. Men ran to the next gap, but because of their panic they did not bring the portable bridge. In the black night dozens of Spaniards tumbled into the waters. Those who managed to cross the gap did so by stepping on the bodies of their comrades.

Finally Cortés and the survivors reached the town of Tacuba at the end of the causeway. Fighting continued but the intensity of the battle ebbed. More than four hundred Spaniards were dead. The men either drowned, were killed

The tree under which Cortés wept after barely escaping Tenochtitlan. (*Library of Congress*)

by arrows, or they were dragged off by the Aztecs to be sacrificed. Thousands of Tlaxcalan allies also were killed. Only about twenty horses survived. Almost all the looted treasure was lost.

Contemplating the tragedy on the causeway, Cortés leaned against an enormous tree and wept. It was June 30, 1520, a night which would forever after be called in Mexican history *La Noche Triste*, The Sad Night.

Historic Tree

The tree under which Cortés wept on The Sad Night still stands in Mexico City. Near the Popotla subway stop, in the Tacuba neighborhood, is an ancient and twisted tree of a type which in Mexico is called the Ahuehuete. It is the same tree where Cortés rested and cried some five hundred years ago. Today the tree is a fire-damaged hulk surrounded by an iron fence, but it is a monument in Mexican history. It is known as the *Arbol de La Noche Triste* (Tree of The Sad Night).

EIGHT

The Conquest of the Aztecs

A lesser leader than Cortés would have mourned his dead, nursed his wounded, and made his way home after such a massive defeat as the Spanish suffered on the Sad Night. But Cortés believed the battle on the causeway was a setback and a learning experience. He was determined to conquer Tenochtitlán and establish a Spanish empire in Mexico.

First he must resupply and rest his troops. Cortés ordered his men to march to Tlaxcala, home of his loyal allies. The men, all of whom were bloody with wounds, obeyed. Along the way they ate wild cherries. They had no other food.

At the town of Otumba on July 7, 1520, the Spanish force halted. Spread out on a cornfield before them was the largest force of Aztec warriors anyone had ever seen. Gómara wrote, "it is affirmed that there were two hundred thousand Indians in the field at Otumba."

Some Spaniards dropped to their knees and prayed at the sight of the huge enemy army. They asked God to receive them in heaven because certainly they were going to die on this dusty field. Others wept upon seeing Aztec soldiers covering the ground. Cortés shouted orders. He assembled the foot soldiers in their tightly packed square formation with spears and swords protruding outward like the quills of a porcupine. The twenty-odd horsemen rode the flanks of the square ready to charge when Cortés commanded.

Shouting war cries, both sides closed for battle. Though the Aztecs were far more numerous than the Spaniards, only a limited portion of them could engage the Spanish ranks at the same time because the soldiers stood side by side in a disciplined European-type formation. At one point in the battle Cortés recognized the Aztec commander by his feathered

The Indian warrior chiefs were easily identifiable by their elaborate headpieces.

headdress which stuck up above the crowds of fighting men. Spurring his horse forward, Cortés cut the man down with his sword. Without a leader the Aztec attacks faltered.

Against staggering odds the wounded and exhausted Spaniards won the Battle of Otumba. Mostly it was the iron will of Cortés that carried them to victory. As Gómara wrote, "Never had there been a more notable feat of arms . . . all the Spaniards who that day saw Hernando Cortés in action swear that never did a man fight as he did, or lead his troops, and that he alone in his person saved them all."

After the Battle of Otumba, the Spaniards crossed mountains, and on July 9, reached Tlaxcalan territory. Now, finally, they could recover from the ordeal of war. The Tlaxcalans

Depiction of Spanish army fighting Indians at the Battle of Otumba

Upon being welcomed by the Tlaxcalans after the Battle of Otumba, Cortés presented the headdress of the Aztec commander he killed as a gift to to the Tlaxcalan leaders.

greeted them like old friends and gave them food. Cortés treated the Tlaxcalan chiefs with utmost respect. Without Tlaxcalan support the Spanish conquest of Mexico would have been impossible.

Cortés allowed his soldiers to rest, but he was eager to move. Ambition burned in his soul. Fiercely he drove himself and his men to prepare for the next mission of conquest.

He began his campaign on September 4 against Tepeaca, a fortified town allied with the Aztecs. After a brief battle the town surrendered and Cortés punished the people with a ruthlessness that surprised even those who knew him. The Tepeaca residents had been read the *requirimiento,* and were Spanish citizens whether they wanted to be or not. By fighting Cortés they defied the king. The men and women were branded on the face with branding irons and then sold into slavery. This terrible penalty was in compliance with Spanish law. Beyond the law he threw some of the town's leaders to his pack of huge wolfhounds. A new Spanish word, *"aperrear"* (to throw to the dogs), came into use under Cortés. The dire punishment inflicted on Tepeaca sent a message to other towns and tribes: Join the Spanish crusade against the Aztecs or you too will suffer.

Cortés's good fortune returned in the months before his final march on the Aztec capital. Several ships carrying soldiers and guns docked at Veracruz. The ships were sent by Cortés's rival, Diego Velásquez and the soldiers aboard were supposed to wage war against Cortés. Once more the soldiers were easily persuaded to switch sides and become part of the Cortés's army.

Other ships came from Spanish-held Caribbean islands with goods to sell or trade. To buy the items he needed, Cortés issued a highly unpopular order: All men who salvaged some gold from the Sad Night must now turn it over to their commander. The men grumbled, but most complied. Cortés used the gold to buy horses and gunpowder.

Cortés's luck took an unexpected twist in the form of a disease. Unknown to the Spaniards a scourge had broken out among the Aztecs. It is widely believed that an African member of the Narváez expedition had the disease smallpox. The man died, but not before he passed on his sickness. The family in whose house he stayed caught smallpox, and then

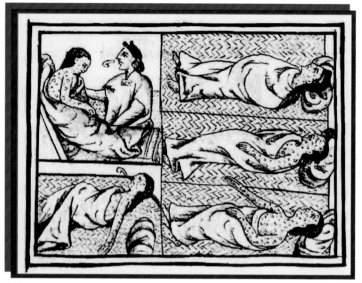

Smallpox, carried to the Americas by the Europeans, ravaged the Aztec people.

a neighboring family, and then another and another. When left unchecked smallpox germs race from person to person with astonishing speed.

Smallpox had been in Europe for hundreds of years. Over the course of many generations, Europeans developed immunity to the disease. Smallpox left pockmarks on faces and blinded some Europeans, but rarely killed them. The people of the Americas had no such immunities. Smallpox had already broken out in Cuba. Now it began to ravage Mexico.

Curbing a Dreaded Disease

Smallpox was the first major disease that was conquered completely by human effort. As early as 1796 an English doctor, Edward Jenner, developed a vaccine that prevented smallpox. In the twentieth century vaccination programs spread to all countries. The World Health Organization, an agency of the United Nations, declared that smallpox was eliminated in 1980 and the vaccinations were discontinued.

Transmitted through the air, smallpox ravaged the people in the crowded Aztec capital. An Aztec wrote, "a great plague broke out here in Tenochtitlán. It began to spread . . . striking everywhere in the city and killing a vast number of our people. Sores erupted on our faces, our breasts, our bellies; we were covered with agonizing sores from head to foot . . . The sick were so utterly helpless that they could only lie on their beds like corpses . . . If they did move their bodies they screamed with pain. A great many died from this plague."

While the pestilence was destroying life in Tenochtitlán, Cortés made careful plans to attack. He bore in mind the painful lessons he learned on the Sad Night. Never could Cortés forget the hundreds of Indian canoes which came swarming towards the causeways as the Spaniards crossed. The canoes represented the Aztec navy. He needed a European navy to counter the enemy fleet. Just hours after he recovered from his grief on the Sad Night he called for his carpenter, Martín López, a skilled builder of boats.

Martín López was ordered to build sailing vessels. They were to be large and swift crafts called brigantines. With the help of Tlaxcalan laborers, López got to work. A fellow Spaniard said he toiled day and night, "with the zeal of a man who comprehended the urgency of the matter." López built thirteen brigantines, all of them solid boats constructed with heavy wooden plankings. It took 8,000 Tlaxcalan porters to transport the vessels over the mountains and down to the lakes in the Valley of Mexico. Moving the boats was an incredible feat in itself as it meant carrying a navy across mountains.

Before advancing against the capital, Cortés reviewed his forces. He now had nine hundred Spanish soldiers, including

Martin Lopez leads the building of a fleet of ships.

eighty-six horsemen. Of the foot soldiers, 118 were armed with either crossbows or arquebuses, and his army had fifteen bronze cannons. More than 100,000 Indian warriors, mostly Tlaxcalan, served with the Spaniards.

In late December 1520 Cortés reentered the Valley of Mexico. He then proceeded to march around the lake system that enclosed Tenochtitlán. He fought battles, but often the towns on the lakes quickly surrendered to Cortés and his army. The Spaniards had established a reputation as a people not to be trifled with. As Cortés wrote his king, "Every day many provinces and cities, who before were subject to Montezuma, come to offer themselves as vassals of Your Majesty, for they see that those who do are well treated by me, and that those who do otherwise are destroyed one after the other."

Cortés's strategy was slow and deliberate. He completely surrounded Tenochtitlán by securing all the communities on

The Spanish army invades Tenochtitlan *(Courtesy of the Rare Book and Special Collections Division, Library of Congress)*

the lake shores. He also disabled the aqueduct that supplied fresh water to the Aztec capital. Now, isolated by Spanish forces, the Aztec capital could not be resupplied with either food or water.

By April 1521, the last brigantine had been hauled over the mountains and set in Lake Texcoco. With flags flying and cannons blasting out a salute, the Spanish fleet was launched. Each brigantine was about forty feet long and held twenty-five to thirty men. A small gun was fixed to the bow of each vessel. With a full set of sails the boats were driven by the wind and could traverse the waters far faster than Indian canoes which were propelled by paddles. A half-dozen crossbow men served on each crew, making this a deadly war fleet.

Cortés took personal command of the thirteen brigantines. He divided his land army into three units and had them press toward the Aztec capital over the three causeways. The Battle of Tenochtitlán began.

One of the first major skirmishes took place on the lake waters. About five hundred Aztec canoes, loaded with shouting warriors, approached the Spanish fleet. There was no breeze so the brigantines could not use their advantage in speed. Spaniards rowed to keep their vessels out of arrow range from the enemy. Suddenly a strong wind swept over the lake, filling the brigantine sails. Cortés ordered his boats to burst into the packed canoes and ram as many of them as possible. He told the king, "We dashed into the midst of them and broke up numberless canoes and killed and drowned many of our enemies. It was the most wonderful sight in the world to behold!"

The battle gave the Spaniards command of the waters surrounding Tenochtitlán. Control of the lakes was an advantage they never surrendered.

Progress on the causeways was slow. Only eight to ten men could advance in ranks along the narrow land bridges. Spanish horses were ineffective, and Aztec courage rose to soaring heights during the causeway battles. Veteran Spanish soldiers who had experienced European battles marveled at the fearlessness and strength displayed by the Aztecs. The Spaniards advanced on the causeways only to be driven back by charging Aztecs.

When the Spaniards finally broke through and entered the city proper they faced even greater obstacles. Tenochtitlán was crisscrossed with canals. The Aztecs removed the bridges over these canals and defended each one as if it were a castle moat. Medieval-style warfare with defenders fighting until death prevailed in the capital. The Aztecs had little food or fresh water. Many were sick with smallpox. Yet they waged war with spirit and great courage, as if death held little consequence over them.

Rooftops on houses and the flat peaks of pyramids became hazards to the Spaniards. Aztecs gathered on these rooftops and flung stones and shot arrows at the enemy below. The Spaniards used their cannons to destroy the buildings. All wooden buildings were burned when captured by infantrymen. When the Spaniards conquered a stone house or a pyramid, they dismantled the structure with picks so the Aztecs could not retake it and use the roof as a firing platform. Thus began the destruction of one of the world's most beautiful cities.

The battle for the capital was fought house to house and street by street. Aztec soldiers continued to press their relentless charges. Typically the Spaniards seized a small neighborhood one day only to be driven out the next by ferocious Aztec counterattacks. "They came [at us] like mad dogs," said Bernal Díaz.

Looming above all other fears in the Spanish mind was the threat of capture. Being taken alive resulted in death on the Aztec altars. The Spaniards believed such a fate meant a man was double damned. First the prisoner would die the terrible death of having his chest slashed open and his heart ripped out. Then, in the afterlife, God would surely punish him for contributing to idol worship.

Though they fought wildly to avoid capture, scores of Spaniards were seized and dragged to the pyramid tops. Since the fighting now swirled through the city streets Spanish soldiers were afforded the view of their comrades suffering death at the altars. They beheld the ghastly ceremonies with a horrified fascination, as if they were compelled to cast their gaze on the scene. As they watched the great snakeskin drum on the pyramid top beat out its grim message.

Bernal Díaz was one of the soldiers who witnessed the sacrifice of Spanish captives. In a passage of his book, *The Discovery and Conquest of Mexico*, he reported:

> When they got [the Spaniards] up to a small square in front of the oratory, where their accursed idols are kept, we saw them place plumes on the heads of many of them and with things like fans in their hands they forced them to dance before [the statues] and after they danced they immediately placed them on their backs . . . and with stone knives they sawed open their chests and drew out their palpitating hearts and offered them to the idols that were there, and they kicked the bodies down the steps, and Indian butchers who were waiting below cut off the arms and feet . . . and [ate] the flesh.

Hernando Cortés himself almost met death at the altars. The captain led a large force of fighting men pressing down a major street toward the city center. He was trying to join a similar force which was commanded by Alvarado and also attacking the main plaza. A linkup between the two army groups would divide the city into halves. At one point the Aztecs fighting Cortés turned and appeared to flee. Sensing victory, a jubilant Cortés ordered his men to charge. He did not know he was being led into a trap. Suddenly, from both sides of the street, came a great rush of screaming warriors.

Cortés suffered a gash on his leg from an Aztec sword. In a European battle he certainly would have been killed on the spot. But Aztec soldiers were trained to capture, not to kill, and this practice ultimately saved Cortés's life. Dozens of Aztec hands grabbed Cortés and pulled him off his horse. He was recognized by the Aztec commander, who wanted to take him alive and offer him to the gods as the ultimate prize. A loyal soldier named Olea fought his way through the crowd surrounding Cortés and hacked the arm off one of the men lugging him toward the pyramid. After a furious fight, other soldiers managed to free their leader. Olea, the hero, was killed. Cortés lost about forty men. Many of them were captured and taken away to the dreaded altars.

The Spaniards were forced to retreat over the causeways and out of the city. It seemed to be a repeat of the Sad Night. But Cortés, displaying his characteristic stubborn courage, rallied his troops and re-launched his invasion. Using Aztec tactics he also feigned retreat only to ambush his foe. One such ambush near the main market cost the lives of 12,000 Aztecs.

The Aztecs, sick and starving, finally began to weaken. An Aztec writer said, "The people were tormented by hunger, and many starved to death. There was no fresh water to drink . . . The only food was lizards, swallows, corncobs, and the salt grasses of the lake . . . They ate the bitterest weeds and even dirt. Nothing can compare with the horrors of that siege and the agonies of the starving. We were so weakened by hunger that, little by little, the enemy forced us to retreat. Little by little, they forced us to the wall."

By July 24, 1521, Cortés completed his linkup with Alvarado's army, thus dividing the city. Three days later the Tlaxcalans captured Montezuma's old palace. As part of their victory celebration the Tlaxcalans set the building on fire. They also slaughtered every man, woman, and child they found still alive.

High officers of the Aztec nation begged Emperor Cuauhtémoc to seek peace with the Spaniards so as to stop the carnage. He would hear no such talk. Instead the emperor made plans to escape the surrounded capital and carry on a guerrilla war against the Spaniards.

On August 13, 1521, Cuauhtémoc and a few of his loyal followers tried to slip away on a canoe. A brigantine commander named Holguín spotted the vessel and thought it, "appeared to be carrying persons of rank." The canoe was captured and Cuauhtémoc surrendered. With the emperor a prisoner, the bloody battle of Tenochitlan finally ended.

An eerie, almost unreal silence settled over the city. For more than ninety days the capital rocked with cannon fire, the screams of war cries, and the blowing of conch shells which summoned the Aztec soldiers into battle. Now stillness prevailed—a strange condition for those subjected to the thunder of battle for so many weeks. Most important to the Spaniards the great snakeskin drum, which announced human sacrifices, fell silent. Bernal Díaz said, "I again declare [that drum] had the most accursed sound and the most dismal that it was possible to invent."

In the ghostly quiet after the battle, Emperor Cuauhtémoc was taken to Cortés. Bernal Díaz claimed the Emperor said, "I have surely done my duty in defense of my City, and I can do no more and I come by force and a prisoner into your presence and into your power, take that dagger that you have in your belt and kill me at once with it."

Cortés assured the young emperor he had nothing to fear. No harm would come to him. He offered food and suggested Cuauhtémoc rest.

A heavy rain descended on Tenochitlan. The downfall doused the many fires burning in the city, but when the rains finally lifted, a scene of unimaginable destruction spread before the survivors of the siege. More than one-third of the capital's inhabitants were dead. Unburied bodies littered the streets. The stench was sickening. The Aztecs who were still alive, mostly women and children wearing rags, scurried away from the victors like frightened animals.

The city itself, which Cortés once called, "the most beautiful thing in the world," was in shambles. Only months ago Cortés dreamed of presenting this city to his king as if it were a shining jewel. Now mountains of burned-out ruins spilled over onto what had been spotlessly clean streets. The mighty pyramids and castles had been flattened in the fury of war. An Aztec poet, overwhelmed by this spectacle, wrote:

> Broken spears lie in the roads . . .
> The houses are roofless.
> The walls are red with blood.
> Our city, our inheritance
> Is lost and dead;
> The shields of our warriors
> Could not save it . . .
> Weep, weep, our people,
> For we have lost Mexico.

NINE

Building A New Spain

The Spanish soldiers had conquered the Aztecs. True to their creed, the men demanded gold as a reward. Where was the gold left behind during the Spanish army's escape on the Sad Night? That treasure filled almost a full room at Axayacatl's palace. The room was now empty. Where was the gold that many Spaniards tried to carry out of the capital only to be drowned by their efforts? The lake waters along the Tacuba causeway were only six to ten feet deep. Spanish divers searched the bottom, but they could find no ingots. The fabulous treasure once owned by Montezuma and stolen by the Spaniards had vanished.

Cortés faced a mutiny among his own men if he failed to do something to find the whereabouts of the treasure. Some soldiers whispered that he—Captain Cortés—had secretly made off with the gold. Cortés ordered Emperor Cuauhtémoc to be tortured by holding his feet to a fire. He later wrote

Cortés tortured
Cuauhtémoc by
holding his feet
over flames.

he issued this order reluctantly and only to satisfy the lusts of his soldiers.

Despite the cruel torture Cuauhtémoc disclosed nothing as to the location of the treasure. The young Aztec leader was left crippled by the ordeal and walked with a limp afterwards. Four years later Cortés had the emperor hung. This treatment—torture and execution—was given to a man Cortés once promised not to harm.

Cuauhtémoc and the Treasure

Today Cuauhtémoc is a national hero in Mexico. As the last Aztec king, his reign marked the end of the mighty empire. Curiously, his name translates as "falling eagle." It is popularly believed that Cuauhtémoc ordered Montezuma's fortune to be buried somewhere in the city and that he took the secret location with him to his grave. When onlookers in modern Mexico City pause to watch a work crew digging a trench for a sewer line, someone in the crowd will often joke, "Hey, if you find Montezuma's treasure, split it with me."

Montezuma's fortune itself was deceiving. It indicated that Mexico was rich in gold and silver. Actually the land had great mineral wealth, but the precious metals lay deep below the surface and had to be mined. Montezuma's holdings represented nearly all of the gold that had been taken from Mexican soil in the last two centuries. Since the Aztecs did not value gold very highly they did not dig deep for the metal. Large-scale mining for gold and silver would come later, under the Spaniards.

By making demands of frightened peasants the Spaniards did grub together a small cache of gold. From this sum Cortés dutifully sent the king his fifth, the *quintero*. He also took one-fifth of the treasure for himself. High officers got portions of the loot as their share. These divisions meant that the eight hundred-odd soldiers who participated in the conquest received little for risking their lives. Bitterness descended on the Spanish army. Martín López, the shipbuilder, later took Cortés to a Spanish court to demand proper compensation for his services. López lost his case.

The defeat of the Aztecs marked the beginning of a Spanish empire in Mexico. The empire was called New Spain, a name suggested by Cortés himself. Immediately after the conquest, Cortés deemed it his responsibility to lay the foundations of New Spain. But first he had to soothe the resentments burning in the hearts of his soldiers. Having no gold to give the men, he gave them land instead. He did this through a system called *encomiendos* and *repartimientos*. Originally *encomiendos* meant the right to collect taxes from native people, and *repartimientos* included the practice of compelling their labor. For the Indians, the system amounted to land-grabbing and slavery. A Spaniard given an *encomiendo* (a land grant) was allowed to force the people living on the land to work for him without pay. This same system was used to divide land in the Caribbean Islands. Under the new rules the Aztec people became landless and found themselves slaves to the Spaniards.

Six months after the fall of Tenochitlán most of the land in the vicinity of the capital had been given as compensation to Spanish soldiers. Once more Cortés claimed the largest land grant for himself, and he gave great holdings to the officers. Cortés's property was ten times larger than the next officer in line. Common soldiers received large farms or home sites. Still, the soldiers grumbled because the officers were granted so much more land than the men. Indian chieftains, especially among the loyal Tlaxcalans, were also given land grants. The two surviving daughters of Montezuma were awarded large encomiendos under Cortés's orders.

Tenochtitlán was destroyed so completely that Cortés pondered the idea of moving the capital of New Spain to some other locale. Finally he decided to rebuild Tenochtitlán. In the months ahead he and other Spaniards began to call the place *Ciudad de Mexico* (City of Mexico or Mexico City). Ciudad de Mexico came quickly into use because Spaniards had difficulty pronouncing Indian words such as Tenochtitlán.

Cortés threw himself into the task of building Mexico City with the same tireless energy he earlier employed to wage war. Using the Aztec pattern of gridlike streets, he laid out his new town with a church and a broad public plaza in the center. The church was built in the same spot where the pyramid to Huitzilopochtli once stood. The plaza spread out where the Aztec market used to operate. Near the city center rose houses owned by prominent Spaniards. Often the churches and the houses were constructed with bricks taken from ruined Aztec pyramids and palaces.

The City Center Today

Cortés' first church, built on the site of the great pyramid, was torn down in 1573 and construction began on the National Cathedral which now stands on the north side of the plaza. The huge and ornate National Cathedral took one hundred years to complete. The broad plaza is popularly called the Zocalo, and Mexicans regard it as a magical spot. It was here some seven hundred years ago that the wandering Aztec tribe first saw an eagle perched on a cactus while devouring a snake. Today young couples come to the Zocalo to hold their marriage ceremonies because they believe getting wed on the sacred grounds of the plaza will cement their unions. Great parties such as Mexican Independence Day (September 16) are celebrated in the Zocalo. The Zocalo is also the political heart of Mexico. Striking labor unions parade on the plaza and dissatisfied political groups gather there to stage noisy demonstrations.

A new Spanish city rose on the ashes of Aztec ruins. Construction proceeded at astonishing speed. Armies of Indian laborers paved the streets and put up scores of houses, churches, and public buildings. To the workers this vast building project was nothing new. Their fathers and grandfathers had constructed the pyramids of Tenochtitlán using the same work gang methods. Indian tribal leaders supervised the huge crews. The men commonly sang as they toiled.

The size of the work gangs and the rapid pace of Mexico City's construction impressed a visiting Spanish priest:

> More people worked on building the great city . . . than upon

the Temple of Jerusalem in Solomon's time . . . The crowds of people who labored at the projects or carried materials, tribute and food to the construction sites were so thick that one could barely squeeze through the broads streets and avenues . . . They carried everything on their backs. They dragged stones and beams with ropes . . . four hundred men at a time, singing and shouting, with voices that never ceased night and day, for such was then great fervor which with they erected the city in those early years.

Ghosts of Tenochtitlán

In the late 1960s workers digging a subway line in Mexico City stumbled across an Aztec temple and other buildings lying below the ground. Today this archaeological site is called *Templo Mayor* (Main Temple) and is visited by thousands of tourists. Workers found another intact temple nearby and built a subway station around the structure. Now, when passengers wait for trains at the Pino Suárez station, they look across the tracks and gaze at the ancient work once built by Aztec hands. Finding relics of Tenochtitlán beneath the soil of Mexico City is not new. As early as 1790 ditch diggers unearthed a circular calendar stone, weighing twenty-five tons, that was once used by Aztec priests. The huge Calendar Stone is now displayed in the Mexico City National Museum of Anthropology.

A devout Catholic, Cortés believed it was his duty to present the gift of Christianity to the natives of New Spain. He wrote the king, requesting that priests be sent to the land. He insisted that the holy men be common priests, not high-ranking bishops. Cortés believed that foremost church officers tended to be corrupt and addicted to high living.

In 1524 the first twelve priests specifically assigned to New Spain arrived at Veracruz. The number twelve was chosen to symbolize the Twelve Apostles of Christ. Certainly these men were humble. They insisted on walking barefoot all the way to Mexico City. Cortés met the group of priests on the outskirts of the capital. He knelt down and kissed their tattered robes and their bleeding feet. This gesture of humility impressed the Indians, and the status of Catholic priests rose in their thoughts.

Immediately the priests began baptizing the Indians and converting them to Christianity. Priests told the Aztecs and other peoples of the one true God and of the scores of saints and holy figures a proper Catholic worships. To the people of Mexico this religious system did not differ radically from their old practices of worshiping many gods. Thousands of Mexicans converted to Christianity in mass baptismal ceremonies. Still, many prayed to their old gods in secret.

As the priests took their message to all parts of the old Aztec Empire, Christianity spread. A priest wrote his superior, "We are very busy with our continuous and great work in the conversion of the infidels of whom . . . over a million people have been baptized, five hundred temples of idols have been razed to the ground and over twenty thousand images of devils that they adored have been broken to pieces and burned . . . The infidels of this city of Mexico, who in formal times had the custom of sacrificing each year over twenty thousand human hearts to their idols now make their offerings to God instead of to devils . . ."

In their zeal to erase the old religion from the minds of the Mexicans, the priests destroyed many profound works of religious art. Statues were broken or burned. Wonderfully decorated manuscripts depicting Aztec history and the roles played by ancient gods were thrown in bonfires. Many priests respected the great artistic skill displayed by Indian sculptors and painters. But the artists created figures of the devil. Those figures were destroyed.

Thousands of Spaniards arrived in the years following the conquest. Many of the newcomers were racially arrogant. New Spain's society treated white immigrants as a privileged class regardless of their skills or the energy they put into their work. Because of their white skin, the immigrants readily acquired land and Indian servants. A priest complained, "They do nothing but command. They are the drones who suck the honey which is made by the poor bees, the Indians . . . They come out very poor from Spain . . . But in a year they have gotten together more goods than a drone of animals can carry, and they must have the houses of gentlemen."

Powerful army officers came to New Spain with dreams of carving out private empires. Building such personal kingdoms violated Spanish law. Only one man—Hernando Cortés—was in a position to deal with the upstarts. By keeping ambitious countrymen in check, Cortés claimed he was acting in the name of the king. In fact, he was maneuvering to maintain his status as the richest, most powerful man in New Spain.

In 1524 Cortés led an army south to the Honduras where he hoped to capture and punish a man named Cristobal de Olid. Olid had been an officer in the conquest, but now he plotted with Cortés's old enemy Diego Velásquez. Cortés marched his men through thick jungle where they were tormented by mosquitoes. Many sickened and died from diseases. Finally, he discovered Olid had been killed by a mutiny of his own men.

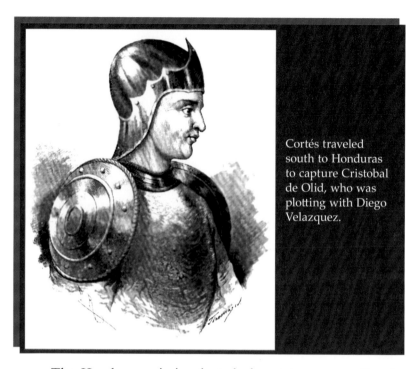

Cortés traveled south to Honduras to capture Cristobal de Olid, who was plotting with Diego Velazquez.

The Honduras mission lasted almost two years. People in Mexico City believed Captain Cortés had died in the southern jungles. One official claimed that in a dream he saw the Captain screaming while surrounded by the fires of hell. When Cortés returned to New Spain's capital he was hailed as a hero, a man who had come back from death and from hell itself.

In the years to come Cortés commanded exploration missions north and south along the Pacific Ocean. Cortés and most other Europeans believed that somewhere in the Americas was a strait, a sea passage that would allow ships to sail from the Atlantic to the Pacific and thus reach the rich lands of China. Cortés searched, in vain, for such a strait, but he made important discoveries. Sailing north he found and named Lower California, which he thought was an island. Many maps today call the waters between Lower California and mainland Mexico the Sea of Cortés. The exception is found on Mexican-made maps where the Cortés name is avoided and the waters are always called the Gulf of California.

The reach of New Spain expanded until it embraced far more territory than did the old Aztec Empire. Eventually New Spain's boundaries stretched south almost to Panama and north to the American state of Colorado. As Spanish explorers and traders ventured into these far-flung lands they brought new crops such as wheat and barley. The burro, which became vital to Mexican farmers, was introduced by early Spaniards.

Donkeys, called "burros" in Spanish, were introduced by the Spanish. *(Library of Congress)*

But those pioneer Spaniards, unknowingly, also took European killer diseases to Mexico. In addition to small-pox, the Spaniards were carriers of diphtheria, measles, and influenza. These sicknesses, long established in Europe, rarely killed Spaniards because of the immunities they acquired over the generations. American Indians had no immunities and European diseases devastated the Indian population.

In the mid-1500s whole towns and villages in New Spain became deserted through the calamity of disease. Death was everywhere. Many Indians thought the end of the world was at hand. A Maya villager noted, "Great was the stench of the dead. After our fathers and grandparents succumbed [to the plague], half the people fled to the fields. The dogs and vultures devoured the bodies. The mortality was terrible. So we became when we were young. All of us were thus. We were born to die."

Population Loss

More than 12 million people lived in what would become New Spain at the time Cortés arrived. Then came the diseases, born in Europe. One hundred years later the population of New Spain stood at about 1.2 million.

Cortés remained the most powerful man in New Spain, but he fell out of favor with the Spanish king. Charles V (1500-1558) was the grandson of Ferdinand and Isabella. He became King of Spain when he was only sixteen. His court teemed with intrigue as the young man often fell under the influence of powerful advisors. Some of those advisors warned the monarch that the ambitious Cortés would usurp royal authority and treat New Spain as his own realm.

Two sordid episodes in Cortés later life marred his reputation. Twelve months after the conquest, Cortés's wife, Catalina, boarded a ship in Cuba and sailed to Mexico. Her arrival was completely unexpected. Cortés had a mistress in his translator, Malinche. He rarely wrote to his wife in Cuba and seldom spoke of her to his friends. At a public dinner to celebrate All Saints' Day the two argued and Catalina was last seen running to her room in tears. She was discovered dead in the morning, and marks along her neck indicated she had been strangled. Cortés claimed his wife died of asthma. Shortly after Catalina's death King Charles sent a trusted agent to New Spain to hold discussions with Cortés. The agent died suddenly and rumors persisted that Cortés had ordered servants to poison the man.

Cortés sailed for Spain in 1528. It was the first time he set foot on his native land in almost twenty-five years. He had left Spain young and almost penniless. Now he returned as a rich man. To demonstrate his wealth he brought exotic goods. His servants included Indian jugglers and acrobats. Also accompanying him were caged jaguars and birds of marvelous plumage. Crowds of peasants followed the Cortés caravan as it traveled. The people delighted in seeing the animals, and in catching a glimpse of the folk hero, Hernando Cortés.

Royal Confusion

Most history books name the king who served in Cortés' time Charles V, which was the title he held when he became ruler of the Holy Roman Empire in 1519. Three years earlier, however, when the sixteen-year-old became king of Spain, his official title was Charles I. Some books continue to refer to him as Charles I.

King Charles V of Spain

The king and the conquistador held several conferences. In meetings Charles V was always properly courteous to Cortés. But the king never granted Captain Cortés the government position he coveted. Cortés wanted to be named Viceroy of New Spain, the highest office that land afforded. He was denied that request, so he returned to New Spain in 1530 a disappointed man.

Cortés further lost prestige in Spain with the emergence of a new and far more successful conquistador. In 1533 Francisco Pizarro conquered the Inca Empire in Peru. Here the Spaniards found the fabulous treasure they had dreamed about from the beginning of their American adventures. Pizarro, whose cruelty was hideous even by conquistador standards, extracted gold and silver from the Incas through a program of torture and murder.

New Spain would eventually prove to have great mineral wealth. In the 1540s rich deposits of silver were discovered in the central part of the country. Zacatecas, about 250 miles northwest of Mexico City, became a major silver mining center. Mines made New Spain the richest silver-bearing land on earth. The few Spaniards who owned the mines grew wealthy beyond their dreams.

While some Spaniards gathered fortunes, Cortés spent his savings. Always

Francisco Pizarro *(Library of Congress)*

restless, Cortés sponsored exploration missions to unknown lands north and south of New Spain. The missions did not reap rewards, and they left Cortés deeply in debt. His attempt to plant a colony in Lower California failed miserably and cost him an enormous sum. To pay back his loans, Cortés sold land. Soon he had given up large tracks of his holdings.

In 1540 Cortés returned to Spain where he hoped to petition the king to grant him a government post in New Spain. Once more the king denied his request. Cortés died in Spain in 1547. At his death he was broken and demoralized, a shell of his old vigorous self.

The city of Zacatecas eventually became a major silver mining center. *(Library of Congress)*

With him died the Age of the Conquistador. It was a time of both excitement and inhuman brutality as men of Spain cast upon the unknown shores of the Americas in the name of God, gold, and glory. By the mid-1500s no more new and rich worlds were discovered and conquered. New Spain was an established Spanish colony, and it would remain under the Spanish flag for the next three hundred years.

TEN

Legacy of the Conquest

In modern Mexico, Columbus Day, held in October, is a grand holiday called *Día de la Raza* (Day of the Race). The "race" refers to the mestizo people. Mestizos are a blending of European and Indian ancestry. The vast majority of Mexicans today are mestizos. On Columbus Day the Mexican people hail Christopher Columbus as the founder of the mestizos. A statue of the great sea captain stands in many Mexican towns, and on his day school children decorate the statue with flowers. Yet Christopher Columbus never set foot on Mexican soil. The true founder of *La Raza* in Mexico is Hernando Cortés. However nowhere in Mexico will one find a statue of Cortés or even a street bearing his name.

Mexican history books brand Cortés as a heartless soldier and a brutal dictator. He tortured people, he executed the popular Aztec leader Cuauhtémoc, and he participated in mass slaughter, particularly at Cholula. His condemnation by Mexican society goes back centuries. Even his bones were cursed.

Twenty years after Cortés's death in Spain, a casket bearing his remains was shipped to Mexico. In his will, Cortés asked to be reburied in Mexico City. His grave was shifted several times. In 1794 New Spain officials decided to place his body under the grounds of the *Hospital de Jesus* (Hospital of Jesus), an institution founded by Cortés shortly after the conquest. The hospital site was appropriate because it was on that very spot where Cortés first greeted Montezuma in 1519.

In the 1820s the people of Mexico rose up against Spain and, after a bitter war, gained their independence. Many leaders of the independence movement demanded that the bones of Cortés—the symbol of Spanish rule—be dug up and burned in a public bonfire. To protect the remains priests reburied the casket in another place in the hospital. It was not until 1946 that the casket was discovered. Cortés's gravesite now draws little attention and is visited only by a few scholars.

Cortés in the View of an Artist

On the east side of the Zocalo in Mexico City sprawls the huge government building called the National Palace. On the walls of that building are murals done in the 1930s by the famous Mexican artist Diego Rivera (1886-1957). The murals depict Mexican history from ancient times. Rivera portrays the pre-Columbian era as a wonderful era when Indians lived in peace with each other and in harmony with nature. Then the Spaniards come. Fierce-looking Spanish soldiers are seen branding Aztec faces with irons. Cortés himself is painted as a grotesque figure who is exchanging gold for Indian slaves. Rivera presents the Spanish conquest as a falling from grace for the Indians followed by a dark and cold period in Mexican history.

A painting of Cortés by Mexican muralist José Clemente Orozco (1883–1949) depicts Cortés as a vicious and demonic figure.

Malinche, Cortés's translator and mistress, is another founder of the mestizo race. As Cortés's mistress, she bore him a baby boy. That boy, Martín Cortés, was born in 1522, and was certainly one of the first mestizos. Malinche herself later married one of Cortés's officers. Through her intelligence and guile Malinche became an influential figure of the conquest period. She achieved power despite the fact that women in the militaristic societies of both the Aztecs and the Spaniards had little voice in making decisions that affected their nations as a whole. Today her name is used scornfully. If a girl prefers American rock music to popular Mexican tunes her friends might tease her and say, "*Tu eres*

Orozco portrays Cortés and Malinche as a sinister Adam and Eve, responsible for taking Mexico out of Paradise.

One of the few statues of Malinche, in Villa Oluta, Veracruz

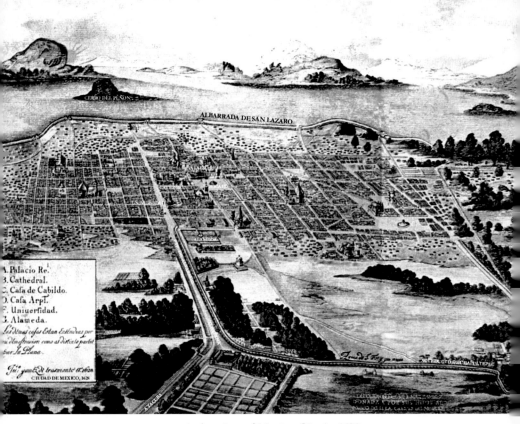

A drawing of Mexico City in 1628

una Malinche." (You are a Malinche), meaning a sellout or a Judas.

The Spanish Conquest (1519–1521) is perhaps the most frequently debated chapter of Mexican history. All students choose their own heroes and villains of the period. With few exceptions the Aztecs rise as heroes while Cortés and the Spaniards are condemned as rogues.

Mexico would not be the country we now know without the influence of Spain. The Spaniards brought their language and their religion to Mexico. Like the mestizo people, today's Mexico is a blending of European and Indian cultures. This blending—this creation—is unique in itself. The uniqueness can be seen in the nation's art, literature, architecture, and music. These creations show a people reaching for a special identity. The Mexican philosopher and Nobel Prize winner

Octavio Paz (1914–1998) said, "The history of Mexico is the history of a man seeking his parentage, his origins . . . He wants to go back beyond the catastrophe he suffered: he wants to be a sun again."

Timeline

1325   Founding of Tenochtitlán and the Aztec Empire.

1480? Montezuma born in the Aztec empire.

1485   Hernando Cortés born in the province of
Extramedura in Spain.

1492   Christopher Columbus discovers land in the
Caribbean Sea.

1502   Montezuma becomes emperor of the Aztecs.

1504   Cortés sails for the New World and settles on
island of Hispaniola.

1508   Spaniards conquer island of Puerto Rico.

1509   Spaniards conquer island of Jamaica.

1511   Cortés participates in the conquest of Cuba.

1517   Francisco de Córdoba leads three Spanish ships
from Cuba on an exploration mission to Mexican
coast.

1518   Juan de Grijalva explores Yucatan region with
a small fleet of ships.

1519   Aztecs await the coming of the god Quetzalcóatl,
as legends say the god will return this year (the

year One Reed on the Aztec calendar).
February—Cortés leaves Cuba commanding a
fleet of eleven ships.
March—Cortés defeats Tobascan Indians on
the Mexican mainland.
April—Spanish ships drop anchor at the port
of Veracruz; Cortés meets with Aztec
representatives.
June—Spaniards officially found the city of
Veracruz, first permanent Spanish settlement
in Mexico.
August—Cortés begins march toward the
Aztec capital.
October—Spaniards slaughter as many as 6,000
people at the Battle of Cholula.
November—Cortés enters Tenochtitlán; Cortés
takes Montezuma prisoner.

1520   May—Soldiers sent by Diego Veláquez land
in Veracruz to arrest Cortés; Lieutenant
Alvarado left in command at Tenochtitlán;
Alvarado attacks Aztec noblemen at a fiesta,
kills hundreds.
June—Cortés returns to capital and finds his
army trapped inside castle; according to
Spanish accounts Emperor Montezuma
killed when stoned by his own people; Aztec
sources claim he was executed by three Spaniards;
on La noche triste Cortés and his army flee
Tenochtitlán, are attacked by Aztecs; four
hundred killed.

July—Cortés defeats Aztec army at Battle of Otumba.

September—Smallpox breaks out in Tenochtitlán, killing thousands; Cortés begins march back to the capital; conquers the city of Tepeaca.

December—Cortés reaches the Valley of Mexico.

1521 April—Spaniards launch fleet of thirteen brigantines in the lake waters surrounding Tenochtitlán.

July 24—Spanish forces meet in Tenochtitlán, dividing the city into halves.

August 13— Cuauhtémoc, the last Aztec emperor, captured; battle for Tenochtitlán ends.

September—Rebuilding of the capital (now called Mexico City) begins; region claimed by Cortés is now New Spain.

1524 First twelve Catholic priests officially assigned to New Spain arrive.

1528 Cortés returns to Spain for the first time in almost twenty-five years.

1530 Cortés returns to New Spain after being denied a government post by the king.

1533 Francisco Pizarro conquers the Incas in South America.

1547 Cortés dies while in Spain.

Sources

CHAPTER ONE: City of Dreams

p. 13, "we were amazed . . ." Bernal Díaz del Castillo,
The Discovery and Conquest of Mexico
(Cambridge, MA: Da Capo Press, 2003), 190.

CHAPTER TWO: The Aztec World

p. 15, "There [in Aztlán] they feasted . . ." Jonathan
Kandell, *La Capital: The Biography of Mexico City*
(New York: Random House, 1988), 26.

p. 18, "And when [the Aztecs] arrived . . ." Ibid., 27.

p. 24, "The city is spread out . . ." Jon Manchip White,
*Cortés And The Downfall of the Aztec
Empire* (New York: Carroll & Graf Publishers, 1971), 99.

p. 24, "My very loved and tender . . ." Ibid., 114-15.

p. 25, "We only came to sleep . . ." Hugh Thomas,
*Conquest: Montezuma, Cortes, and the Fall
of Old Mexico* (New York: Simon & Schuster, 1993), 309.

p. 28, "Here is my well-beloved . . ." White, *Cortés and
the Downfall of the Aztec Empire*, 120.

CHAPTER THREE: God, Gold, and Glory

p. 30, "the most distinguished . . ." Thomas, Conquest, 62.

p. 36, "They had little wealth . . ." Francisco López de
Gómara, *Cortés: The Life of the Conqueror by His Secretary*
(Berkeley: University of California Press, 1964), 7.

p. 36, "He was the source of trouble . . ." Ibid., 8.

p. 37, "Cortés was nineteen . . ." Ibid., 9.

p. 37, "The sailors were filled with . . ." Ibid., 9-10.

p. 38, "Amongst them the land . . ." Thomas, *Conquest*, 65.

p. 38, "They [the Spaniards] make bets . . ." Kandell, *La Capital*, 86.

p. 40, "[Cortés] extracted a great deal . . ." Gómara, *Cortés*, 11.

p. 43, "they attacked us hand-to-hand . . ." Díaz, *The Discovery and Conquest of Mexico*, 12.

p. 44, "México. México." Hammond Innes, *The Conquistadors* (New York: Alfred A. Knopf, 1969), 43.

CHAPTER FOUR: The Lure of Mexico

p. 45, "Who could conquer . . ." Thomas, *Conquest*, 5.

p. 46, "a flaming ear of corn," Miguel Leon-Portilla, ed. *Broken Spears: The Aztec Account of the Conquest of Mexico* (Boston: Beacon Press, 1992), 4.

p. 47, "Oh, my beloved sons . . ." Thomas, *Conquest*, 41.

p. 52, "Certain it is . . ." Gómara, *Cortés*, 24.

p. 53, "[Cortés] reprimanded . . ." Díaz, *The Discovery and Conquest of Mexico*, 41.

p. 55, "Our lord and king . . ." Leon-Portilla, *Broken Spears*, 17.

p. 55, "large greyhound . . . came up to them . . ." Gómara, *Cortés*, 38.

p. 58, "Hear us, o God . . ." Kandell, *La Capital*, 97.

p. 59, "I and my companions . . ." Ibid., 98.

p. 59, "A thing like a ball . . ." Leon-Portilla, *Broken Spears*, 30.

p. 61, "when the chiefs and the . . ." Thomas, *Conquest*, 213.

p. 62, "The first article presented . . ." Díaz, *The Discovery and Conquest of Mexico*, 74.

CHAPTER FIVE: The March Inland

p. 64, "What men have there been . . ." Díaz, *The Discovery and Conquest of Mexico*, 192.

p. 65, "In my last letter . . ." Harry M. Rosen, ed., *Conquest: Dispatches of Cortés From the New World* (New York: Grosset & Dunlap, 1862), 22.

p. 65, "We came here to serve God . . ." Kandell, *La Capital*, 89.

p. 66, "Well, [the Spaniards] must be . . ." Thomas, *Conquest*, 235.

p. 67, "All the plain was . . ." Díaz, *The Discovery and Conquest of Mexico*, 130.

p. 68, "How they began . . ." Ibid.

p. 68, "Whose arms were weary from . . ." Thomas, *Conquest*, 245.

p. 69, "I even heard . . ." Rosen, *Conquest: Dispatches of Cortés*, 30.

p. 69, "The lords of Tlaxcala . . ." Gómara, *Cortés*, 118.

p. 69-70, "There is a market . . ." Rosen, *Conquest: Dispatches of Cortés*, 31.

p. 73, "more beautiful than anything . . ." Thomas, *Conquest*, 259.

p. 74, "[they] remained some distance . . ." Díaz, 171.

p. 75, "we did such an execution . . ." Rosen, *Conquest: Dispatches of Cortés*, 35.

p. 75, "The Tlaxcalans went about . . ." Díaz, *The Discovery and Conquest of Mexico*, 179.

p. 77, "The common people were . . ." Leon-Portilla, *Broken Spears*, 41.

CHAPTER SIX: Cortés and Montezuma

p. 78, "two very high and marvelous . . ." Rosen, *Conquest: Dispatches of Cortés*, 37.

p. 79, "as good as the best in Spain . . ." Ibid., 40-41.

p. 80, "Like monkeys they seized upon . . ." Thomas, *Conquest*, 269.

p. 82, "I do not know how to describe . . ." Díaz, *The Discovery and Conquest of Mexico*, 191.

p. 82-83, "so many people were crowded . . ." Gómara, *Cortés*, 140.

p. 83, "richly dressed" Rosen, *Conquest: Dispatches of Cortés*, 41.

p. 84, "No, it is not a dream . . ." Leon-Portilla, *Broken Spears*, 64.

p. 84, "[F]rom what you tell us of your . . ." Rosen, *Conquest: Dispatches of Cortés*, 43.

p. 85, "Then the Spaniards fired one . . ." Leon-Portilla, *Broken Spears,* 66.

p. 86, "goldsmiths in Spain, inasmuch . . ." Thomas, *Conquest*, 22.

p. 88, "the Indian women who . . ." Díaz, *The Discovery and Conquest of Mexico*, 214.

p. 88, "birds which have feathers . . ." Ibid., 212.

p. 88, "was horrible to listen to . . ." Ibid., 213.

p. 90, "It had a very broad . . ." Ibid., 219-220.

p. 90, "Señor Momtezuma, I do understand . . ." Ibid., 220.

p. 90-91, "if I had known. . . " Ibid., 220-221.

p. 92, "I took it for certain . . ." Ibid., 226.

CHAPTER SEVEN: The Captive Nation

p. 95, "of good height and well . . ." Díaz, *The Discovery and Conquest of Mexico*, 208.

p. 95, "No prince in all the world . . ." Rosen, *Conquest: Dispatches of Cortés*, 60.

p. 96, "The Spaniards grinned like . . ." Leon-Portilla, *Broken Spears*, 68.

p. 100, "They surrounded those who danced . . ."
Thomas, *Conquest*, 389.

p. 101, "[It] should have made . . ." Ibid., 393.

p. 103, "I declare that I do not know . . ." Díaz, *The Discovery and Conquest of Mexico*, 302.

p. 103, "one of his [Montezuma's] own subjects . . ."
Rosen, *Conquest: Dispatches of Cortés*, 72.

p. 107, "so those who died died rich . . ." Gómara, *Cortés*, 222.

CHAPTER EIGHT: The Conquest of the Aztecs

p. 109, "it is affirmed that there were . . ." Gómara, *Cortés*, 225.

p. 111, "Never had there been . . ." Ibid.

p. 115, "a great plague broke out . . ." Leon-Portilla, *Broken Spears*, 92-93.

p. 115, "with the zeal of a man . . ." Thomas, *Conquest*, 443.

p. 116, "Every day many provinces and cities . . ."
Rosen, *Conquest: Dispatches of Cortés*, 82.

p. 118, "We dashed into the midst . . ." Díaz, *The Discovery and Conquest of Mexico*, 403.

p. 119, "They came [at us] like . . ." Ibid., 410.

p. 120, "When they got [the Spaniards] . . ." Ibid., 436.

p. 121, "The people were tormented by . . ." Leon-Portilla, *Broken Spears*, 107-109.

p. 122, "appeared to be carrying . . ." Thomas, *Conquest*, 525.

p. 122, "I again declare . . ." Díaz, *The Discovery and Conquest of Mexico*, 441.

p. 122, "I have surely done my duty . . ." Ibid., 453.

p. 123, "the most beautiful thing . . ." Thomas, *Conquest*

p. 123, "Broken spears lie . . ." T. R. Fehrenbach, *Fire and Blood: A History of Mexico* (New York: Macmillan, 1973), 146.

CHAPTER NINE: Building A New Spain

p. 128-129, "More people worked on . . ." Kandell, *La Capital*, 129-130.

p. 130, "We are very busy with . . ." Enrique Krause, *Mexico: Biography of Power*, trans. Hank Heifetz (New York: Harper Collins, 1997), 34.

p. 131, "They do nothing but command . . ." Fehrenbach, *Fire and Blood*, 181.

p. 134, "Great was the stench of the dead . . ." Kandell, *La Capital*, 155.

CHAPTER TEN: Legacy of the Conquest

p. 145, "The history of Mexico is . . ." Octavio Paz, *The Labyrinth of Solitude* (New York, Grove Press, 1985), 20.

Bibliography

Díaz, Bernal del Castillo. *The Discovery and Conquest of Mexico.* Cambridge, MA: Da Capo Press, 2003.

Fehrenbach, T. R. *Fire and Blood: A History of Mexico.* New York: Macmillan, 1973.

Gómara, Francisco López de. *Cortés: The Life of the Conqueror by His Secretary.* Translated by Lesley Byrd Simpson. Berkeley: University of California Press, 1964.

Innes, Hammond. *The Conquistadors.* New York: Alfred A. Knopf, 1969.

Kandell, Jonathan. La Capital: *The Biography of Mexico City.* New York: Random House, 1988.

Krause, Enrique. *Mexico: Biography of Power.* Translated by Hank Heifetz. New York: Harper Collins, 1997.

Leon-Portilla, Miguel, ed. *Broken Spears: The Aztec Account of the Conquest of Mexico.* Boston: Beacon Press, 1992.

Paz, Octavio. *The Labyrinth of Solitude*. New York:
Grove Press, 1985 edition.

Rosen, Harry M., ed. Conquest: *Dispatches of Cortés
From the New World*. New York: Grosset &
Dunlap, 1962.

Thomas, Hugh. Conquest: *Montezuma, Cortés, and the Fall
of Old Mexico*. New York: Simon & Schuster, 1993.

White, Jon Manchip. Cortés And The Downfall of the Aztec
Empire. New York: Carroll & Graf Publishers, 1971.

Web sites

www.ambergriscaye.com/pages/mayan/aztec.html
The Aztecs Speak—An Aztec Account of the Conquest of Mexico

www.ucalgary.ca/applied_history/tutor/euvoya/aztec.html
European Voyages of Exploration: Aztec Empire

www.worldbook.com/features/cinco/html
Spanish Conquest

Index